HUMANIZING CHANGE: A JOURNEY OF DISCOVERY

Eight Principles for Acquiring
True Personal and Professional Alignment
in Our Lives

Travis Sample

University Press of America,® Inc.
Lanham · New York · Oxford

Copyright © 2002 by
University Press of America,® Inc.
4720 Boston Way
Lanham, Maryland 20706

PO Box 317
Oxford
OX2 9RU, UK

ISBN 0-7618-2429-4 (paperback : alk. ppr.)

To Barbara,
for sharing your love and moral support,
and for putting up with me.

CONTENTS

PREFACE

Man is what he makes of himself. And the courage to be oneself is the courage to make of oneself what one wants to be.

— Paul Tillich

In an era of increasing societal turbulence and an apparent and alarming insensitivity to the critical and fundamental aspects underlying how we must embrace and celebrate change to our lives, as well as in organizations today, we continue to struggle with balancing the view of accepting greater demands upon us with the desire to focus upon what truly gives our lives meaning, purpose, and relevance. It remains my firm belief that we are in a state of denial as a society, for we suffer from a *deprivation of meaning* in our lives. And what do I mean by meaning? Let me share the insight of Leo Rosten: "I cannot believe that the purpose of life is to be happy. I think the purpose of life is to be useful, to be responsible, to be honorable, to be compassionate. It is, above all, to matter; to count, to stand for something, to have made some difference that you lived at all."

Ideas can open our minds, if we choose to be vulnerable and have a willingness to grow; grow emotionally, intellectually, and spiritually. It's my sense that too many of us are locked away in our separate realities, our parochial loyalties, our fixed ways of seeing ourselves as strangers. And our apparent and continued fascination and dependence on television to connect us to the outside world only strengthens those walls we have created around us. Ideas can liberate us from the barriers we have created. In the passion of a teacher, and sharing is the essence of teaching, I have studied, researched, and am sharing with you, my readers, in my little book,

rich insights which I believe to be valuable as you understand the importance and power of discovering what our lives are about. For truly every
decision we make, whether it be significant or rather insignificant, stems
from how we find meaning and purpose in our lives.

Change is happening so rapidly, and globally, that our institutions are
not keeping up. Change has a rigidity about it, because you're moving so
quickly that the area in which you can see things is limited. However,
Heraclitus said; *"Life itself is change."* Literally, nothing remains static for
an instant, from a planetary to a molecular level. Many of us are like an
individual trying to dance a jig on a log in a river. We've become so
preoccupied with dancing on the log that we don't see the waterfall ahead.
The result, predictably, is we keep doing that same thing more frenetically,
like we're in a groove, reacting to others' expectations and assumptions
upon us. To truly value and embrace change, I suggest a different perspective, to help us discover meaning and purpose in our life. Too many of us
have just accepted things as they are without retaining a passion and desire
to be a better person, and to leave a better society than the one we were
born into.

Humanizing change is essentially committing oneself to self-change.
Too many of us look for easy solutions to embracing change, looking in the
wrong places. There really are no magic pills, magic pins, slogans, or magic
plans. It is also much more than just being self-responsible. It goes to a
deeper level. We must acquire an appetite for self-accountability and must
avoid people who do not share this view, for they reflect a negative synergy
and deny us our creativity, our imagination, our curiosity, our awareness,
our fascination with the human experience. And it is only those who
understand the power of serving, serving the larger good, the larger
community, who truly have their spiritual needs met and experience a life
fulfilled. And it remains my belief that our spiritual needs, as contrasted
with the other three needs that we experience daily (psychological, social,
and financial) ... that make the miracle of the human experience truly
worthwhile.

Following the example set by successful *self-changers*, my *humanizing
change principles* will expose you to the power of learning and actualizing
new skills, drawing upon your inner strength, enhancing your *self-
sufficiency, self-reliance, self-confidence* ... and avoiding becoming
dependent on others for solutions. As behavioral psychologist B.F. Skinner
once remarked, *"One thing wrong with the Western world is that we too
often help those who can help themselves."*

Far too many of us seem to be obsessed with individualism ... and a degree of selfishness ... reflecting a "me-ism" that has, for at least some four decades, corroded our institutions and created a misalignment in our lives. If you are interested in maximizing your own self-interest, how can you think about the other person to whom you're supposed to be committed? Carl Jung, the prominent psychologist, stated, "in the final analysis, we count for something only because of the essentials we embody, and if we do not embody that, life is wasted." What essentials might he be talking about? My book on the eight principles of *becoming before we do* speaks to those essentials, principles which clearly can be used in both our personal, as well as our professional lives.

It is my firm belief that organizations cannot be transformed and effectively process accelerating change until and unless each of us commits ourselves to personal transformation and servant leadership, anchored in a deep belief in the power inherent in living a life of integrity and honor, while we effectively pursue both personal and organizational alignment.

It is my goal, in writing this book, to both inspire and provoke you to create your own legacy, your own destiny, while discovering an inner strength that will guide you as you achieve greatness in your life. Each chapter will provide necessary tools which will be helpful as you analyze your chosen roles during this journey.

Having said that, and as a humble academic, I'm reminded of the story of the fifth grader, giving an oral report in her history class on the great philosopher Socrates. She said, "Socrates was an old person that went around giving people advice, and they poisoned him." So, not wanting to be poisoned, I'll be judicious in giving out advice.

This book had its beginnings some ten years ago, and, while I have taught this material, made literally hundreds of public speeches, and written dozens of articles on the subject, it has taken me this long to finally acknowledge and to act upon the encouragement of my friends and professional colleagues to put these thoughts into a book. And, not insignificantly, I have been so inspired from my many students who have supported and believed in me and the passion I have for teaching. This has been life's joy. Dr. Karl Menninger told us that "The friends who listen to us are the ones we move toward, and we want to sit in their radius. When we are listened to, it creates us, makes us unfold and expand."

I am so blessed; blessed with a loving and supportive family, having led what some might see as an alternative life style, being married some sixty years to the same woman, thirty years apiece; blessed to have a wonderful son and daughter, a terrific son-in-law and a gorgeous granddaughter who is just too beautiful to behold. Their presence in my life has been the primary experience in providing the strength and passion to put my thoughts into this little book. Their warmth, their support, has convinced me in the power to live life to the fullest, everyday; for tomorrow, today is gone, never to be re-cycled, re-lived, impossible to be re-purchased. We have one shot to pursue greatness today. For everyday… is truly a blessed and great day.

I feel so honored and privileged to have served in my country's military forces, where I was truly grateful for every day of the twenty-six years I proudly wore the Air Force uniform. It was then, and remains today, a true love affair. I recall vividly the day I joined the military. My mom had asked if she could go with me down to the Military Induction Center in Houston. I said, "sure." Several times, as we were driving downtown, she repeatedly said, "Are you certain you want to do this?" I said, "Mom, if I were anymore confident in this decision, I wouldn't be able to stand it."

My worst fear that day was that I was not going to be good enough to be accepted to join the Air Force. I felt fortunate and truly privileged when I received official notice that I was selected to attend the Air Force Officer Training School at Medina Base, Lackland, San Antonio, Texas. I also feel blessed to have been chosen to teach and serve my students, at Shenandoah University, for the last twelve years. Their continuing challenges keep me young.

Many of my professors at the University of Southern California (USC) were instrumental and so supportive of my insight and passion to pursue these issues I am sharing with you. Let me acknowledge the Chairman of my Dissertation Committee, Dr. Ronald Stupak, who believed in my believing in myself. He always reminded me to believe in the power of overcoming one's fear of failure; Dr. Chet Newland and Dr. Cynthia McSwain (now at George Washington University), for their probing, pushing, and challenging me to be my best … everyday. Other USC professors whom I owe a great deal of appreciation include Dr. Joseph Wholey, who told me, quite accurately, upon receiving one of my earliest papers in his Public Policy class: "Mr. Sample, this is not a distinguished effort." And Dr. Chet Newland, whom I was fortunate to have on my Dissertation Committee, always reminding and pushing me … to commit myself to true excellence, excellence in research, as well as in critical thinking. They always had a way of putting things in perspective and that uncanny ability to remind their students of the importance of humility in their classes. Since those rather "intimidating" moments, which I remember vividly, even after some 18 years, I would like to think I have improved my intellectual depth and writing skills. I wish also to acknowledge "Team America," a group of men whom I was very close to during the four years I attended USC as a doctoral student: Drs. Roger Gilbertson, George McAleer, Frank Gavin, and Al Beck.

I wish to thank Dr. James Davis, the President of Shenandoah University, for his trust and faith in me, when he offered me the opportunity to join the Harry Byrd, Jr. School of Business back in 1990. And special thanks to Dr. Joel Stegall, recently retired, Shenandoah's Vice President for Academic Affairs, and Dean Stan Harrison, of the Byrd School, for their unwavering support. And special thanks goes to my dear friend at Shenandoah, Ralph Lewis, who tragically died from cancer two years ago. His life epitomized the power of *servant leadership*. And, I wish to add, not insignificantly, the support I received in the Fall of 2001 from the Dean of the School of Business, Al Akhawayn University, Ifrane, Morocco, Dr. Ahmed Driouchi, which allowed me the freedom and resources to complete my manuscript.

Obviously, without the faith and support of my publisher, University Press of America, and their professionalism, this journey would not have been possible. Special appreciation also goes to my manuscript editor, Dr. Joanne Jacobs, Assoc. Prof. of English, Shenandoah University; and Ms. Susan Spencer of the University of California Law School, Berkeley, for her technical skills in assisting in text design, preparation, and printing.

Furthermore, I am indebted to Major General Jacques Paul Klein, USAF, Ret.d, a great American, currently NATO's Commissioner in Bosnia, and one of my heroes. Jacques was a gentleman to whom I reported for a couple of years when I was a rather young Lieutenant Colonel. I remember the day when I received my acceptance to attend, in residence, the Industrial College of the Armed Forces, Washington, D.C. I expressed my disappointment and told Jacques I had wanted to go to its sister school, the National War College, and was unsure if I should accept the assignment or not. He was very firm in urging me to accept and told me it would be a life-changing experience. I did accept the assignment, attended; and discovered, as always, he was right.

I am one of the luckiest guys around, truly blessed with so many friends and associates who have had faith in me, provided wise counsel, and have given so much emotional and spiritual support throughout my professional career with the Air Force, General Electric (GE) Corporation, and

Shenandoah University. I could not have achieved this *journey of discovery* without them. I am forever grateful to my close and valued friend, Dr. Bob Swezey, a true warrior, whose courage and determination to overcome the scourge of cancer has been inspirational for so many of his loved ones.

Let me not fail to recognize one of my colleagues and senior managers with GE's Space Systems Division, with whom I worked very closely, Harry Tucci. Harry, whom I definitely owe an intellectual debt, always believed in creating your own destiny. As a former Marine, he was passionate about life, and taught me not to take life casually; to *grab it by the throat and hang on.* Harry was driven by the pursuit of excellence in his life, and expected it from those around him.

I firmly believe, as the great Althea Gibson once reminded us, that *"what do we live for, if not to make life less difficult for each other?"* I dedicate this book to those individuals whose inspiration, trust, and support made it possible, especially my Mother, whose love was unconditional, who always told me, *"Many things in life will catch your attention ... but only a few will really be heartfelt. It's not what we see that truly counts. It's ultimately our heart. Find something that you truly love to do. Follow your dreams. That's what you should do."* Mom, I am forever thankful for that advice; the same advice I have shared with my children.

My little book represents a journey of risk, love, truth, courage, and individual growth. And, to that end, it remains my belief that we must reflect upon and look at different paradigms, different approaches, on how we relate to meaning and purpose in our professional lives. We must resist relying on living our lives solely based on how we feel. Rather, we should reflect upon, discover, or *recover* what our life's *meaning* is ... what we "actualize,"act upon, essentially what we *DO*. We need to consider and internalize who we *ARE*, and what we need to *BECOME*, as human beings. Ultimately, life is not about how many "toys" we accumulate, but what our life's purpose is. What gives us meaning in life? Is it something that comes from outside us—or is it something to be discovered—that is within all of us, within all of us already? I suggest it is the latter. We must choose to recover it, to embrace it—and to celebrate it.

Dear God,

Please show me how to discover true meaning and purpose in my life and then how to achieve true humanness; the becoming—which is the most challenging and difficult stage; then I can do, I can be,

I can acquire personal mastery—which then becomes the easiest stage to conquer. (Travis Sample)

These brief thoughts, captured in my *eight principles*, are shared with the intent to connect with those who are eager to search for the best that life has to offer and who have chosen not to die before they have discovered, truly developed, and released their potential for loving themselves, loving and serving others, and those who have acquired an appetite for pursuing *personal mastery.* This project, this research of how each of us can choose to create our future, our destiny, our legacy, is very real to me. If, after you read my book, and you are sharing its principles with others, they might say, "My friend, you're dreaming." You should reply, "Thank you. You've made my day."

This effort, culminating after some dozen years of research and commitment to organizational behavior and theory literature, has been an immense joy for me and is truly from the heart, my gift to you. I have attempted to merge practical approaches with the passion of *possibility*, which I believe essential today if we have a chance to fulfill our dreams of living a marvelous, fulfilled life. It is not meant to be scripture. If I wrote this book one year from now, it likely would be a bit different. For I would be a different person, having experienced another twelve months of my life. But, at this moment in time, I am not saying *this is the way it is.* I am saying *this is the way I see it.* Now, let me invite you to join me in this journey of discovery. Like all of life, there may be a few *potholes and bumps in the road*, but I have laid out a sequential, rather linear, process which will take you to a new, higher level of *self-discovery and self-management*; and a greater appreciation for and respect for one's humanness, as we experience the miracle of life.

Travis Sample
June 2002

PERMISSIONS

Permission from Tyndale House Publishers, Inc. for Bible verses taken from the *New Living Translation*.

Permission to use quotations from Joel Barker, Stephen Covey, Margaret Wheatley and Warren Bennis.

Cover design by Getty Images.

INTRODUCTION

Life is not so much a problem to be solved, as a mystery to be lived.

— *M. Scott Peck*

The theme of my book, *Humanizing Change: A Journey of Discovery*, has likely been discussed many times, in many classrooms, in many colleges and boardrooms throughout this land. While it is found in primal wisdom traditions, in modern indigenous tribes, and in most spiritual thought, I was first exposed to this thought as a young college student. My fraternity motto was *Esse Quam Videri*, "To Be ... Rather Than To Seem." I confess I really didn't appreciate it so much then, but I do now; for I firmly believe life is born from an unquenchable need to find true *meaning* in our lives which leads to the human quest to *be: the being stage, then we become a new person; the becoming stage...* then we *actualize* through free choices and free expression; to the next stage, which is to *do;* then we *become* again. This cycle, this process, never truly stops, even after our death, for those that we have influenced, through their choices, can emulate this powerful approach to how one lives their life.

One of the most widely used change processes, consciousness-raising, was first described by Sigmund Freud, who said, "*The basic objective of psychoanalysis is to make the unconscious conscious.*" But, how do we do this? I suggest by knowing ourselves, by experimenting with what I refer to as *self-liberation*, an acknowledgement that you are the only one who is able to respond, speak, and act for yourself. Do we truly understand the process of *human change*? My sense is that studying history, physics, and ecology will certainly help us understand these phenomena. But we're either too lazy, arrogant, or too ignorant. However, as the psychotherapist Paul Watzlawick compellingly puts it,

> *If that little man from Mars arrived and asked us to explain our techniques for effecting human change, and if we then told him, would he not scratch his head (or its equivalent) in disbelief and ask us why we have arrived at such complicated, abstruse, and far-fetched theories, rather than just first of all investigating how human change comes naturally, spontaneously, and on an everyday basis.*

Let me offer, for reflection and consideration, a paradigm shift that captures, depicts, and illustrates a human growth cycle/process that you might want to study/actualize as you pursue excellence and alignment in your life. I believe it powerfully, and compellingly, speaks to the importance of *BECOMING ... BEFORE ... WE DO!*

Sequential Stages of How One Acquires
True Personal and Professional Alignment

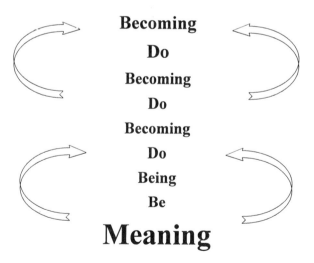

Becoming

Do

Becoming

Do

Becoming

Do

Being

Be

Meaning

> *We would rather be ruined than changed. We would rather die in our dread than climb the cross of the moment and let our illusions die.* (W. H. Auden)

The approach to *humanizing change* I am speaking about is not the latest fad, prescription, or flavor of the month, or the most recent "hot ticket" to come along as we struggle with the increasing stress and turbulence in our daily lives and in our professional pursuits. And it will not be presented in a manner which one finds in certain rather popular "show business celebrities" who raise the intensity/energy in an auditorium with slick, artificial, "motivational" gimmicks, not unlike the snakeoil salesmen of years ago; presentations where one is "pumped" briefly, but after a couple of days—or hours—returns to their office or home, and forgets everything they were exposed to. That approach reminds me of having a terrific Chinese meal; then, just after a few hours, you become quite hungry all over again.

I suspect everyone that reads my book will be struck with the knowledge that so little of this information is really new. We know this approach; we know this material already in our hearts, but we don't live it. We just know it. Your Mom told you about this stuff. But I am going to come at you very forcefully, using words to probe, provoke, push, pull, and challenge you to look deeply into your heart, into your soul, for that *fire within*, which we all possess, and to believe in your ability to pursue and acquire greatness in your life. Then, you must choose to act. The greatest benefit you will derive from from reading my book and experiencing this journey is that it will greatly enhance the quality of all of your relationships, certainly, foremost, the one you have with yourself.

Undoubtedly, many of you who have chosen, at least, to read my preface, are thinking , "I learned that. I learned about how we can modify our behavior personally, how organizations must transition, about the accelerating pace of change in society today, and how we can deal with it." What I am sharing with my readers is really known to all of us already; it lives in our very blood. It has been recorded in history, literally going back to Egyptian writings found in the "Wisdom of Ptah-Hotep" in 2500 B.C.E., which significantly affected Greek culture. Also relevant are Eastern "wisdom literature" found in the writings of Confucius (6th Century B.C.E.) and Mencius (4th Century B.C.E.). It is found in many chapters of the Bible; specifically in the books of *Job, Proverbs, and Psalms,* and is woven throughout the diaries and journals of our Founding Fathers, e.g., Benjamin Franklin's *The Art of Virtue and The Autobiography of Benjamin Franklin*. This put in place the American experiment in self governance, based on the concepts of dispersal of power, equality for all, individual opportunity and responsibility, and the belief in God's gift of inalienable rights, an experiment which has lasted for over two centuries and has so dramatically and significantly influenced many, if not most, of the world's countries.

But too many people are still in denial, either unwilling or unable to internalize what we already know. We know that to find "meaning" in our lives and then to realize our humanness, which is to "be" (our "being") before we choose to "do", then to "actualize and operationalize" (the "becoming" phase) is to discover—to believe—in the miracle of the human spirit. To recognize the miracle of the interconnected and interdependent eco-systems in nature, we must not exclude human beings from this universal and self-affirming equation. But, even when faced with empirical evidence, we remain in denial. E.M. Hallowell of the Harvard Medical School, states; *"Virtually everyone I see; I counsel, is experiencing some deficiency of human contact.... People feel lonely, isolated, or confused at work."* Categorizing it as toxic worry, Hallowell states; *"even brain chemistry has shown the debilitating effects of partial isolation."* James Hillman, in his bestseller *The Soul's Code* proposes that "our calling in life is inborn and that it's our mission in life to realize its imperatives." My sense is that all must know this in our deep, inner life. But, for whatever reason, we resist its true wisdom and power. So, what is there to do?

What can we do to regain our balance, our alignment, while continuing to *prefer the comfortable "lie" to the uncomfortable truth with respect to the potential power within us*? We choose not to believe in the vast power that we waste in our personal lives, that so damages the potential strength and joy of relationships, and is certainly lost in our professional lives as well. The result has been centuries of wasted talent, wasted intellectual capital, and a landscape replete with corrosive and destructive relation-ships. *In life, the issue is not control, but dynamic connectedness.* (Erich Jantsch)

I am not an expert on *humanizing change*, nor do I think there are any. Along with my professional colleagues, I am struggling and groping with this issue. However, I am very attentive to the literature, and I am sure you agree; current thinking is replete with research and study of the potential value, the potential harm, and impact of organizational restructuring, thoughtless downsizing, ill-advised mergers, even hasty bankruptcies. Now, make no mistake about it. Sometimes, significant interventions and resource decisions are very necessary and appropriate in this highly competitive world. But we have to clearly redefine what "job" security and stability mean. Your deep security resides within you; it is not external. Nor should your security rest on your insistence on always being right. It's perfectly okay, and emotionally mature, to admit, on occasion, when you're wrong. Celebrate those moments.

These disruptive activities, with literally millions of people impacted, are taking place throughout the industrialized as well as many developing countries. And what is the predictable outcome? After a typical downsizing, or "right sizing," survivors become narrow-minded, self-absorbed, and risk averse. We fall back on centralization; we tend to stop investing in responsible and accountable strategic planning, innovation is curtailed, scapegoating becomes rampant; then, predictably, serious resistance to change occurs. What morale might exist disappears. Productivity lessens and the culture of distrust is magnified. Many of the organizational change initiatives are not evaluated rigorously and often have unintended consequences. However, it remains my belief that "cosmetic" changes won't work. Blaming others or some event is irresponsible, and denying accountability is immature.

We have to change the way we think as people, as citizens. I don't believe anything really changes until ideas change. Thus, we must change our paradigm, or our map—and we can change our world. Disappointments, setbacks, obstacles, and discomfort are part of the human experience. But, I know no one who has achieved any degree of success or greatness in his or her life, that who has not overcome significant adversity. Discover that *"fire within"*; commit yourself to greatness. Do not limit yourself to the expectations and assumptions that others place on you. You have a huge reservoir of potential that is literally "untapped." Overcome any internal resistance to pursue personal mastery in your life. I suggest that you believe in yourself; believe in those whom you trust; believe in the power of investing in relationships; choose to diagnose from the "outside," but rely on the strength of your "inner" power, your personal alignment; choose to say what you think, and choose to do what you say; choose to live a life committed to *service to others*, one of interdependence; then you will experience true freedom and the joy of a new life.

No matter where it's from, it's there ... the Spark.... That tells me I'm somebody of Value, Worth, and Meaning. Oh, I'm put down, called worthless, treated that way, too, until I believe it ... almost; but then there's the Spark. Sometimes I think it's gone out, completely, or never was there. And then somebody touches me with a smile, or a word, or a deed. and, the Spark rekindles and burns—sometimes for only a moment—but I remember that I'm somebody of Value, Worth, and Meaning. Not as I seem, even to me, but better, much better; capable of so much more, of things no one else can do. And the vision I once saw of myself as good, even great—the vision I thought was lost—is relit by the glow of the Spark. And for a moment—sometimes for only a glimpse, I see and feel the truth; that I'm somebody of Value, Worth, and Meaning, by the light and the glow of the Spark. (D. H. Groberg)

While I am writing this Introduction to my book, we have, as a nation, as a world, been impacted powerfully by the Sept. 11th terrorist attack on America. Terrorism's gravity, its geo-political, psycho-social, economic, emotional, spiritual, and financial effects have yet to be fully realized. But, along with other freedom-loving people in the world, we are strong and resilient; we will ultimately prevail in this battle against "cancerous" evil. I remain confident a peaceful community of nations can be achieved. We are on this earth to support each other, to make life easier for each other, to respect the uniqueness and contributions of all people, and to accept the absolute certainty that we share the same fate as all humans on this earth.

However, along with many of my professional colleagues, I believe we are also in a different type of crisis, a crisis of major dimensions. Prior to the tragic September 11th terrorist attacks on the World Trade Center and the Pentagon—and there were ominous signs as early as late Fall 2000—our economy was slowing down. But it is clear that this terrible, horrific incident did accelerate the weakness of our economy. And, while I believe our economic strength will improve—even dramatically—by the last quarter of 2002, I believe it will take longer for our spiritual debt; our spiritual recession, to improve.

My eight principles are not just casually identified, nor are they in any random order. They are sequential in nature. If you do not get *Principle* #1 down pretty solidly, you will never get to *Principle* #2. In fact, *Principle* #1 is the *mother of all principles*. In Chapter 1, I explore *Principle* #1, how and why we must choose to discover, to recover, our inner core, *what our life is about,* which defines who we are and what brings meaning, relevance, and purpose to each of us. Only then can we *choose* to believe that a life of fulfillment and true joy is possible. Too many people do not believe this. Too many people do not believe they can choose to control their lives. As I share my second *Principle* in Chapter 2, *find that something you love to do; then, you will never work again.* You may choose to affiliate with many organizations, many communities, where you share your talents, your imagination, your creativity; but you are responsible for yourself. Choose to change your paradigm, your mental map. You "work" (I hate that word) for no one but yourself. Choose to acquire an appetite for accountability and interdependence. Chapter 3 speaks about the power of successfully pursuing and acquiring *servant leadership,* serving the larger community, providing a model of self-management and visionary leadership that I believe is the optimum model if one has any chance to achieve their highest potential in life. Chapter 4 includes the results of my research which shows that true personal and professional effectiveness relies upon *giving power away,* not holding on to it.

Chapter 5 explores the power inherent in *defining one's priorities in life,* for so many things we do are essentially unimportant, they are not in alignment with our chosen values and principles. Doing these things essentially wastes valuable energy and innovativeness. Chapter 6 speaks about the *importance of mutual trust,* about holding ourselves and others not only responsible, but accountable as well. Accountability is not solely for the "little people." It must be a contract that reflects *mutual accountability.* Chapter 7 explores the power and strength not only of valuing ... but also of truly seeking and *celebrating differences in our lives.* My final principle, in Chapter 8, *acquiring an appetite for personal mastery,* encapsulates and rewards your successful journey of effectively accomplishing the seven principles which precede it. Goethe remarked that *"our greatest happiness lies in practicing a talent that we were meant to use."* My Chapter 8 integrates the previous 7 principles into a much higher level of living, truly, one of approaching self-transcendence. It essentially reflects the *true power of choice.* For it is not "paying the price" of living the first seven principles, but truly *enjoying the marvelous benefits,* of living the first seven habits.

> *Life seeks organization, but it uses messes to get there. Organization is a process, not a structure. Simultaneously, and in ways difficult to chart, the process of organizing involves creating relationships around a shared sense of purpose, exchanging and creating information, learning constantly, paying attention to the results of our efforts, co-adapting, co-evolving, developing wisdom as we learn, staying clear about our purpose, being alert to changes from all directions.* (Margaret Wheatley)

Look around you; you see people in organizations, choosing to, ostensibly, defend themselves, by denying others the psychological air of freedom to choose. They create constipating policies, rules, structures, which impede communication and deny one a sense of value, trustworthiness, self-worth, and self-esteem. This has clearly taken a severe toll on the American workforce during this past decade. Now I say people in organizations because organizations don't do anything. They make no decisions. It's people who do; and, quite often, insecure people, individuals who are scripted/conditioned to use the pardigm of "management over, power over, or control over," rather than the more courageous and mature paradigm of "power with": servant leadership. *An organizational system is a set and pattern of participation processes very different and aside from the solid structure of steel, brick, and mortar buildings that house these behavioral activities.* I share the view of Yvonna Lincoln, who describes organizations as being "interconnected like a vast network of interference patterns." Individuals in organizations who choose to respect and recognize how to use power and influence ethically in relationships are the key to the power of *humanizing change*. Their lives in the workplace must be redefined. These *servant leaders* will provide a sense of freedom which is vital to a culture that creates and nurtures positive relationships, lubricating the appetite to grow emotionally and spiritually, certainly acquiring technical competencies/skills, but allowing all to choose to grow emotionally and spiritually as well. I cannot make it any more clear than that.

And we say, "Yeah, I know that. I am aware of that. I learned that. I believe that." But we still really choose not to believe in the power of personal choice, the power to create our own destiny, our future, and, yes, our legacy. And there still remains an absence of courage from individuals who choose not to believe they are indeed responsible for their futures, not their employers, not their government, not their spouses, not their teachers. I know many of you reading my book have plastered your walls with certificates signifying your completion of training seminars that symbolize that you've learned this, but, have you really learned anything at all? I'm glad I asked.

The following "signature" story I believe captures what I mean by truly learning something. It's a Saturday morning at the Apple Blossom Mall, in Winchester, Virginia. And a gentleman is walking around with a cocker spaniel. A youngster, about ten years old, walks up to him and says, "what a cute dog." "What is your dog's name?" The man says, "My dog is named Barnaby." "Wow! What a cute dog," says the boy. "Does Barnaby know any tricks?" "Does Barnaby know any tricks?" "Barnaby knows dozens of tricks." "Can Barnaby do some tricks for me?" "Oh, no," says the man, "Barnaby doesn't do tricks, he just knows tricks."

So, what's the moral of the story? If there is no action, there is no learning. And in the 21st Century, because of global competition, the accelerating, truly dizzying pace of change, powerful new technologies, and the fact that the rules have changed in today's workplace, the covenant has been broken. Just working hard will no longer bring job security. For one's deep security rests within us; it is not external. Just knowing the tricks is not good enough; you have to "do tricks today." (*I'm reminded of the question regarding five frogs sitting on a log and four decide to jump off. How many are left? Five are left. Deciding to jump off is not jumping off. You have to do it and do it today.*)

I agree with the famed Professor Emeritus Leo Buscaglia, the "love doctor" of the University of Southern California, who said, "*Learning is the greatest adventure in the world ... because it's the process of becoming.*" Every time we learn something new, we become something new. The cycle continues until our death. Today, learning is clearly the currency of the future. Intellectual capital is today the dominant competitive weapon, the "force multiplier" in today's global marketplace. Thus, the challenge, according to Warren Bennis, is how to develop an organization's social architecture so that it actually generates this capability.

I am a different person today for having shared these thoughts with you today, and I readily admit, there is a risk in doing this. Professor Buscaglia reminded us that to expose feelings is to risk your true self. To place your ideas and your dreams before others is to risk being called foolish or naïve. I am confident, on occasion, I have been called worse. (Thomas Jonathon "Stonewall" Jackson, one of the legendary heroes of the Confederacy, said, "*Never take counsel of your fears.*") We are inheriting a world where ceaselesss creative self-expression, and embracing and celebrating relationships, are life's organizing energies; where there is no such thing as a separate human being, and all are leaders. Choose to grab the gold ring. Refuse to be solely a consumer of the natural gifts of our society. Share the joy with others around you. Commit yourself to pursuing greatness by serving others, by lifting their spirits. It's really a different way to live one's life:

Becoming ...becoming. Life is on its way to further complications, further deepness and mystery, further processes of becoming and change. Life is circles of becoming, an autocatalytic set, inflaming itself with its own sparks, breeding upon itself more life and more wildness and more "becomingness." Life has no conditions, no moments that are not instantly becoming something more than life itself. (Kevin Kelly, *Out of Control*)

I learned a long time ago that nobody has ever taught anything to anybody. I could be the wisest man in the world and tell you all that I know, but if you don't want to know it, internalize it, and actualize it, you will not learn it. We do not learn from being told. Knowledge does not equal behavior, and telling does not equal doing. It's a discovery process; and we discover when we're ready to discover—and not before. Marcel Proust reminds that "the real act of discovery consists not in finding new lands ... but in seeing with new eyes."

Saying that, what I am going to attempt to do in this book is ask that, in your mind's eye you visualize a screen, full of dots. This journey will challenge you, provoke you, inspire you ... and, as you connect these dots, you might feel a bit emotionally and intellectually uncomfortable. For most of us are indeed scripted or conditioned to seek comfort. And you may conclude that your life is without purpose, without meaning. I believe the purpose of life is to live a life of purpose, committing oneself to the larger good, something that we move toward together, in conversation. We define it as we go along. I think it's been very well said that the common good is the good we seek in common. The larger good is what's good for all of us as a whole, not just what's good for one or another individual.

It's my observation that we rather enjoy stability and security. But, I submit, as Dr. Margaret Wheatley has repeatedly told us, "If you are into stability and comfort, you are a danger to yourself, your family, and your organization." To truly acquire greatness in your lives, you must quite often *become comfortable with discomfort* and accept the view that anxiety and guilt are your friends when you discover freedom. I share the view of the popular author Gail Sheehy, who reminds us that, *"Growth demands a temporary surrender of security."*

Most of the chapters in my book include many true events in my life; these I define as "signature stories." It's my belief that we all have signature stories; but, unfortunately, most of us die with them still within us, never being fully expressed, interpreted, or thoroughly explored. Many of us, reluctant, insecure, shy, or ashamed keep our signature stories private, fearful of ridicule. This is a sad loss for all of us. For we need to be courageous and speak our stories; we need to be heard as we move toward the wholeness of integrity and humanness. To share with others is how we connect in relationships.

> *Without exposing ourselves; without the vulnerability, the telling, without the hearing and processing of others' stories, we are left with ugly, frayed holes in the fabric of our lives ... valued pieces torn from the web that connects us one to the other* (Margaret Wheatley).

Speaking, connecting, sharing and listening move us closer together. The released secrets are vital threads that strengthen that bond, that connect relationships, one to another. I also include in my book a number of classic movie scenes that capture and underscore—compellingly—cogent issues relevant to the theme of my research in *humanizing change.*

When we achieve true alignment in our lives, we are able to integrate the spirit—our connection with that which is greater than ourselves. We acknowledge that we simply are ... in all of our uniqueness ... one with all, sharing the same fate. Thus, the constancy of change: ebbing and flowing ... always transforming ... always becoming, always seeking to accurately interpret our perception of reality.

> *Since we cannot change reality, let us change the eyes through which we see reality.* (Nikos Kazantzakis)

The true signature events I share in the chapters capture the foundational behavioral aspects, which I believe crucial as we explore key pieces to this puzzle I call *humanizing change.* My eight sequential stages are steps which one can choose to embrace, stages which capture what I believe the essence of becoming; a necessary state before we have any chance at all to acquire greatness in our lives. I believe these principles have been growing in the consciousness of humans for many centuries, certainly since the invention of the printing press in the 15th Century. They are not entirely new ideas, but I believe them to be self-affirming and truly universal. And, comcomitantly, I believe violating these principles will surely jeopardize one's likelihood of living a self-fulfilling life, both personal, as well as professional.

Humanizing Change does not come from a "slogan of the month"—or a speech at the annual staff retreat. It happens when people choose to transform themselves by embracing certain principles which bring true meaning and purpose into their lives. *Organizations do not behave. People behave—by choice—in certain ways.* And, if you think my principles are "touchy feely," lacking in structure and discipline, you are wrong. I suggest a belief in, and acting upon, these principles ... requires far greater discipline and structure in one's life, not less. But to effectively embrace and celebrate the principles is, in a way, not unlike becoming a competitive marathon runner. It's difficult at first, taking quite a bit of time, energy, and self-discipline to strengthen sufficiently your cardiovascular system to be able to complete a 26-mile run. One will struggle at first; the body will resist. But then the body strengthens itself. It becomes resilient to the significant stress placed upon it. And then you break through the artificial barrier that holds you back. Then the marathon becomes truly a joyous experience. And, having competed in a Marine Corps Marathon, years ago, I can attest personally to this marvelous adventure.

Dr. Leo Buscaglia died four years ago; an extremely prolific and successful author, he was a real treasure, teaching some of the most popular classes at USC. He said that *"learning is the greatest adventure in the world—because it's the process of becoming."* Every time we learn something new, we become something new. I'm a different person today for sharing the thoughts in my book with you. Reaching out to you, the reader, means I am taking a risk. To hope is to risk despair; and to try, to risk failure. But risks must be taken, because the greatest risk in life is to risk nothing. The person who risks nothing does nothing, has nothing, is nothing, and becomes nothing. You may avoid suffering and sorrow, but you simply cannot learn and feel and change and grow and love and live, if you do not risk. One must be vulnerable today to achieve greatness.

> *This above all: to thine own self be true, and it must follow, as the night the day, thou canst not then be false to any man.* (William Shakespeare, Hamlet)

I firmly believe if you do not acquire and nurture an appetite for things that challenge existing paradigms, you do not grow; you do not grow intellectually, emotionally, or spiritually. If I am successful, you will be a different person when you finish reading my book. I know I am a different person for sharing these thoughts with you. This journey will guide you through an *experience* of personal growth; it will open a door for you, but you must choose to enter it by yourself.

My invitation to you to join me in this journey of discovery is sincere, truly quite simple, and one of an appreciation for the brevity of one's life. Don't waste your life doing the same things over and over, expecting different results. It won't happen. See the world anew. If you think about it, there really are just two essential variables with respect to how one determines and chooses their future, their destiny and their legacy: determine what you want to become and how much you want to invest to make that dream come true.

See your life as a true present, a gift from God. You never asked to be born. You didn't have a vote. Apparently, native-born citizens of America had roughly only a 4% chance of being born in America. Ninety-six percent of the inhabitants on this earth did not have a vote either on where they were to be born, or where they would live their lives. Unlike those living in many of our 240 countries on the earth, we in America truly have glorious opportunities to be great or to be mediocre, a victim, wallowing in self-pity. Choose the former.

At the end of each chapter, you will be given a short quiz which invites you to reflect on what you have read and introduces you to the next principle. You have now finished my Preface and Introduction. Before you read my *first principle, the mother of all principles,* ask yourself, now, what is your life about? On a scale of 1-10, a self-assessment of 1 would be a sense of confusion, disillusionment, disengagement, disconnectness, and deep insecurity. A grade of 9 or 10 reflects a life of true fulfillment, one of alignment. You know what your life is about. Your deep security and spirituality rest within you. They are internal. You wake up every morning choosing to take it with you, not unlike your weather and to connect with others, loved ones, colleagues. Is there true balance in your life— emotionally, psycho-socially, spiritually? Do you feel valued, affirmed, appreciated? If not, why not? I invite you to read and study chapter one, my *first principle,* and reflect back on this little quiz. Has there been enlighten-ment? Have you grown intellectually, spiritually, emotionally? Think. Think hard. Enjoy.

1

KNOW WHAT YOUR LIFE IS ABOUT

This is the true joy in life, being used for a purpose recognized by yourself as a mighty one. Being a force of nature instead of a feverish, selfish little clod of ailments and grievances complaining that the world will not devote itself to making you happy. I am of the opinion that my life belongs to the whole community and as I live, it is my privilege—my privilege to do for it whatever I can. I want to be thoroughly used up when I die, for the harder I work, the more I love. I rejoice in life for its own sake. Life is no brief candle to me; it is a sort of splendid torch which I've got a hold of for the moment and I want to make it burn as brightly as possible before handing it on to future generations.

— George Bernard Shaw

When I was a young, very young man, somewhere around eleven-years-old in fact, I started my professional career, working after school selling subscriptions for the *Houston Press,* a newspaper that has long since gone out of business. Around 3:30 p.m. everyday, I would meet my crew chief, at a location just a short walk from my elementary school. My crew of some 6 or 7 guys would be driven to a residential community, where we would be given a certain route, and we would go door to door, asking the residents if they would be interested in subscribing to the newspaper. We also worked on Saturdays, but only from nine to noon, working in pairs, one young man on either side of the street. Now, this job wasn't for the faint of heart, because, as you might imagine, it could be, on occasion, a bit humbling, painful, even punishing because of the many rejections we would get. Being a "door to door" salesman can be literally cruel and inhuman punishment. It was 1951, and while we received only about twenty-five cents for every subscription we would write, that was pretty serious money for an eleven-year-old.

I recall those early days as if they were this week. I was paired with another youngster from my fifth-grade class. Now I had practiced and rehearsed what I would say at the doors for hours before that first day. But I was still terribly nervous, not sure if I could do this or not. But the big moment came—absolutely "cold turkey." And not having had much training (in fact, none) I was "thrown to the wolves to sink or swim." I memorized my sales pitch. If a child came to the door, I would ask if their Mom or Dad were home. And, if an adult came to the door, I would say; "Hello, Mam (or Sir), I'm Travis Sample, a student at Eleanor Roosevelt Elementary School. By chance, do you subscribe to the *Houston Press*?" Then, depending on the response, I would either thank the person politely and leave, or I would quickly move into my "spiel" about how terrific it would be to subscribe to a great city newspaper.

I was a pretty stubborn young man. That first day on the job, I knocked on every door, choosing not to skip even one house. But it became very clear, very early, and I was advised by the crew chief, that I had to have a thick skin. He said some people would scream at me, slam the door in my face, and just be very unpleasant. He was right. One even asked their dog to chase me out of their yard. One man cursed me and told me to get lost. Well, I chose not to let the cursing bother me, and I felt reasonably confident that I wasn't lost, so I just pressed on. And, after awhile, I didn't take it personally. Well, after an hour or so, I hadn't even come close to getting one subscription. But I remained passionate and optimistic in my goal, my goal to succeed. For me, failure was not an option. I was mindful of a famous line, attributed to Winston Churchill; "Real courage is going from rejection to rejection in one's life, and never losing one's enthusiasm." And one of my crew chiefs at the *Houston Press*, who was one of our favorites, handed out a little pamphlet to us one day that included the following inspirational wisdom:

In Africa, a gazelle wakes up every morning knowing that it must run faster than the fastest lion, or else it will be killed. Every morning a lion wakes up knowing it must run faster than the slowest gazelle, or it will starve. It doesn't matter if you're a lion, or a gazelle; when you wake up, you had better be running.
(Author unknown)

I took this to heart—then—and everyday since. I woke up, and in my household, everyone woke up early. You put your clothes on, and you start running. So, I pressed on every day, oblivious to the string of rejections and negative reactions I was getting from my soliciting job. But, my late father had always told me that to stay in alignment, to stay centered, "the main thing... was to keep the main thing ... the main thing, and everything else will be a piece of cake." While I never quite understood what he was talking about, I knew that with only a sixth-grade education, and with all of his obvious faults, my dad was a pretty smart guy. Later, I realized the key was defining or discovering what the *main thing* is.

I was absolutely determined to keep knocking on those darn doors, even when I became terribly thirsty and even when my right-hand knuckles started to ache and swell. I chose to be relentless, tenacious; I refused to give up, no matter how many people said "no," literally turning a deaf ear to rejection. I just believed I was responsible for my life, my future, my destiny, and I was never one to just give up.

You are the DIRECTOR in your life. Now, write your script.
(Michael Todd)

As we approached some three hours on our route, and it was an unusually hot day in Houston, my buddy across the street, came over to me, and said; "Travis, I can't do this anymore. I just can't go on. This is terrible. I'm going to go back to where we are to meet the crew chief and wait for you." If I recall, he did give up permanently, and told the crew chief that he just wasn't cut out for this sort of thing. He actually chose not to even come back the second day.

Now, I continued on. I had to go on. I believed I had no choice. (Looking back at the time in my life, I realize now I did make a choice—the right one). And, although I didn't realize how poor I was at the time, looking back on my life then, my family, which included three brothers, was truly blessed in spirit, but we were "seriously" poor. At this time in our lives, we had no running water in the house and relied on a portable toilet out back. All four of us boys slept in one bedroom. And, although my father was a hard worker, his steady employment as a truck driver, even with his overtime, barely provided a liveable wage. My mother worked part-time at a local laundry, washing and ironing people's dirty clothes. It was very clear that money was scarce, and I didn't want to be a financial burden on my parents, so I had to work to bring in additional money for the family. But, as the saying goes, there is always a silver lining. Mine was that I was the number two boy; thus, I would get the "hand-me-downs" of my older brother, which wasn't too bad. Sometimes the clothes wouldn't fit just right, because my older brother was four inches taller than I, and about forty pounds heavier, but it was okay. I didn't complain.

So, I pressed on. I never quit, or even, for a moment, thought of quitting. I became quite passionate, persistent, and skilled in my sales pitch, and became somewhat of an accomplished door-to-door salesperson. I even convinced myself that meeting the hundreds of different types of people—happy people, drunk people, angry people, caring people, hateful people, confused people, weird people, people with varying moods—was a privilege. I was getting a terrific education, being exposed to all these differences. I convinced myself that I was one of the luckiest guys around. It just couldn't get much better than this. I was confident that the subscription sales eventually would start coming in, and, they did.

Over the weeks, months, and years, I started making, for me at that time, a good salary; sometimes, fifteen or twenty dollars a week. That first payday, which I received about two weeks later, on a Saturday morning, earned me $8.50, cash money. I opened up that small white envelope and held those dollar bills; WOW! What a thrill for an eleven-year-old kid. I was so excited, and I remember vividly on the way home, that, somehow, I wanted to treat myself to something special. I did. I splurged on a banana split, paying for it with my own money. I think it cost thirty-five cents, big money back in 1951. That was freedom. And, in those days, without video games, and with the movies costing nine cents for admission, it was pretty easy to save your money. It wasn't too many months before I had saved enough money to make a down payment on the purchase of a set of World Book Encyclopedias. Even today, I can close my eyes, some fifty years later and can still smell the freshness of those brand new books when I brought them home. My curiosity and love for reading was very strong, and I read those encyclopedias every day, eventually, numerous times, literally from cover to cover.

After the *Houston Press* closed its doors, I started selling subscriptions for the *Houston Post* and stayed with that for a number of years, until I entered the University of Houston, where I "graduated" to working at the local gas station, with a guaranteed wage of sixty cents per hour. Actually, that was pretty good money in 1960. But, I still have fond memories of those days of selling newspaper subscriptions. It certainly made one appreciate the power of passion and humility.

> *The essence of passion—passion is powerful—nothing was ever achieved without it, and nothing can take its place. No matter what you face in life, if your passion is great enough, you will find the strength to succeed. Without passion, life has no meaning. So put your heart, mind, and soul into even your smallest acts.... This is the essence of passion. This is the secret to life, and to its meaning.*
> (Author unknown)

T.S. Eliot reminds us that "it is not enough to understand what we ought to be, unless we know what we are; and we do not understand what we are unless we know what we ought to be." As we begin this journey together, you must know my perspective, my paradigm, my set of cognitive filters. It is my firm belief that who we are ... what we stand for, and what we are, speaks far more eloquently and compellingly than what we know and what we do. My ongoing thought is, with just a little effort, you can *choose* to *be* now what you truly desire to *be in the future. But you must choose to believe in the possibility of possibilities.*

I suspect everyone knows that marvelous, joyous feeling of falling in love with another person. But not everyone is exactly familiar with feeling that wonderful emotion over your "job." However, that is exactly the passion, the joy, I am referring to, which is necessary if you have any chance to acquire greatness. Patricia Boverie and Michael Kroth, in their recent book *Transforming Work* refer to this as achieving *occupational intimacy.* They speak of three balanced components: work you love to do, work that is meaningful, and a work environment that is nurturing. Is this possible? I not only think it possible; I think the future workforce in America will demand it.

> *To feel joy requires a decision on our part—it is a chosen approach to life, a chosen attitude, a chosen awareness.* (Jaroldeen Asplund Edwards)

For most of history, earning a living, or "working," was something one had to do because, after all, you had to eat. Life, for the vast majority of the populace, did not have much leisure to it, at least not how we define leisure today. Now many people still allow their "work" to consume their lives totally: that's where they get their energy, how they define enjoyment. But, historically, it wasn't intended that an individual should or could enjoy their work. It wasn't expected. Thus, the idea that your employment was supposed to be meaningful just wasn't discussed. Things have changed, and changed dramatically. It is far different today, and the future will bring even greater, more revolutionary changes in what we seek in our lives, what needs we want satisfied, and how we define "work." Today, more and more people look for meaning in their contributions. And they are demanding other types of currencies be provided for their services, not solely money, but demands and benefits that truly never occurred to anyone a century ago.

A very famous American philosopher, Ernestine (Lily Tomlin) created and nurtured a professional comedic career built upon her switchboard operator characterization and one memorable statement: "Is this the person to whom I am speaking?" Well, I believe I am familiar with the person who has chosen to read my book. It's someone who is struggling with the accel-erating, dizzying pace of change in his or her professional life, at a time when the world is truly becoming much smaller, brought on by virtually instant satellite communication and the mind-boggling speed of infor-mation. It's someone who is trying to keep up with new technologies, which increasingly accelerate the "dizzying" rate at which things change.

Along with new workplace stresses; can one just turn their heads and deny that there are major, paradigmatic, revolutionary forces at play in today's workplace as we engage, with some anxiety, the 21st century? So, given the dynamics, the confusion that is happening daily in our lives—personally and professionally—how do we stay in alignment, emotionally and spiritually balanced?

> *The meaning of earthly existence is not, as we have grown used to thinking, in prosperity, but in the development of the soul. (*Alexan-der Solzhenitsyn, *Gulag Archepelego II*)

Accepting the fact that all human beings need both to nurture and be nurtured throughout our lives, which of your behaviors do you value the most? Which behaviors do you value the least? Are you feeling more content and peaceful these days, or more stressed? Are you becoming someone you admire? Where do the answers lie? The following wisdom might help:

> *When you get what you want in your struggle for self, And the world makes you king for a day, just go to a mirror and look at yourself, and see what that man has to say. For it isn't your father or mother or wife whose judgment upon you must pass. The fellow whose verdict counts most in your life is the one staring back from the glass. Some people may think you are a straight shootin' chum and call you a wonderful guy, but the man in the glass says you're only a bum, if you can't look him straight in the eye. He's the fellow to please, never mind all the rest, for he's with you clear up to the end. And you've passed your most dangerous, difficult tests if the the man in the glass is your friend. You may fool the whole world down the pathway of years and get pats on the back as you pass, but your final reward will be heartaches and tears, if you've cheated the man in the glass.* (Author unknown)

I submit that many, if not most Americans, are out of alignment today, no longer "centered" with "balanced" values and principles. We're struggling with competing demands on our lives, financial, emotional, and spiritual—as well as personal and professional. I do not use the word "spiritual" casually. The origin of the word "spirit" reveals the life-giving nature that ancients recognized in it. Descending to English from the Latin *spirare,* it means "to breathe." This is essentially psychological "air" that breathes life into all of us. And *spirituality*—the deeply alive place within each of us that longs for fulfillment, distinct and separate from the word "religion"—causes humans to feel uplifted, causes us to realize our humanness as we connect to a greater order. *Spirituality* is not passive and manifests itself in something as simple as feeling listened to attentively by a co-worker, or when we see a beautiful sunrise. While easier to describe than define, most of us have little difficulty identifying it when we feel it within us.

Deepak Chopra, a physician and popular author on body-mind-spirit relationships, has described *spirituality* as the domain of increased awareness, helping us understand who we are, that deep mystery of our being, and how we *become.* And M. Scott Peck defines *spirituality* in a similar vein ... *the attempt to be in harmony with an unseen order of things.* It is not something that humans have asked for—or demanded—but, it is truly a gift from God. And the new models for understanding nature, reality, and even God are pointing beyond the individual to a kind of interdependent web of becoming, of being.

Many of us live unfulfilled lives, gasping and grasping for what gives our lives meaning and relevance. Too many of us, for example, never overcome the inner struggle between initiative and purpose—and guilt—and inhibition. Choose to overcome this insecurity.

Your life's meaning is not going to come from your company, your spouse, your government, and certainly not from me. It's going to come from inside you. As Oscar Wilde reminded us, "To live is the rarest thing in the world. Most people exist.... That is all." Or the powerful words of Cardinal Newman: *"Fear not that thy life shall come to an end, but rather that it shall never have a beginning."* We all know that determination, dedication, focused energy, and courage appear spontaneously *when we care deeply about something. But first we must choose to care about ourselves.* Elie Wiesel shared this insight regarding taking responsibility for our future, our destiny, our legacy: "Ultimately, the only power to which man should aspire is that which he exercises over himself." Another writer declared:

> *When you empty yourself of who and what you think you are, there is less to lose than you had feared. The degree to which you stop protecting yourself from unpleasant possibilities, emotions, and information ... is the degree to which you can deal with what is real.* (Carol Orsborn)

Thus, the challenge we face today is to discover, not create, that core belief—that *fire within*—that core strength that I believe resides in all of us, but unfortunately lies dormant in too many of us. At Shenandoah University, we say *most people die with their music still in them.* We don't even get close to our highest level of potential. There is a powerful passage in the Gospel of Thomas, one of the Gnostic Gospels, which provides great wisdom: *"If you do not bring forth what is within you, then what you do not bring forth ... will destroy you."* I submit that choosing to read my book will challenge you, provoke you, and expose you to that hidden power of discovering that *one thing* which will provide meaning and purpose in your life, but it will be a journey of discovery—and a journey of recovery as well.

Discovering the *meaning* in our lives is the foundation which all choices stem from. This leads to our uniqueness—the *be*—which is observed as our *being,* our humanness. The *being* leads to actualizing, the *doing.* Then you *become* again—someone new—different than you were previously ... and the cycle of *doing and becoming begins again.*

Given the momentous events and marvelous technological breakthroughs of the past decade, I believe it is time to explore and examine patterns of shared assumptions, expectations, skills, and competencies; time to discover new, innovative ways in which we *self motivate,* pursue and acquire personal alignment, and inspire each other in today's workplace. We must know that relying on past successes to insure future successes is a recipe for disaster. Let me be blunt. *Whatever made you successful will no longer work.* And, it is my intent, with this book, to make it comfortable for you to leave your "comfort zone"; as an analog, not unlike a fetus within the womb, relying on the umbilical cord for its survival, a fetus with some natural reluctance to be born, to be thrown out into this cold, cruel world.

Let me also add that I will do everything in my power, with the use of the English language, to make you uncomfortable if you desire to stay in your "comfort zone." I cannot promise you success, but I can promise you greatness, if you believe; but there will be turbulence. There will be uncertainty, doubt, and chaos; but that is what life is about. *Before the beginning of great brilliance, there must be chaos. (I Ching, 1000 B.C.E.)*

I am human. I am a self-defining value. I can make of myself whatever I choose. (ZULU—African tribe concept of humanness)

Margaret Wheatley shares that "*we notice what we notice because of who we are ... and create ourselves by what we choose to notice. And, once this work of self-authorship has begun, we inhabit the world we have created.*" Thus, we self- restrict/limit/constrict, and this mindset must be broken, if we have any chance at all to acquire and embrace alignment in our lives ... finding that thing we truly love to do in life so we will never have to work again. What I am suggesting is that we must become comfortable while experiencing what we have been conditioned to think of as discomfort. I believe we must redefine the word "discomfort." How strongly do I feel about this? If you are deep into security, into stability, into pursuit of comfort in today's workplace, there is virtually no possibility you will even get close to your highest potential of growth.

It is a dark time when people lack courage because they don't know who they are. (Tran Paul Rein Po Shay—Tibetan teacher)

I know I am saying things that have been said many times over and over. But we don't do it. Either we're not truly listening, choosing to remain in a state of denial, or choosing to find it too uncomfortable to change our mindset. But I feel this subject, this theme, is too important to just push aside. I will continue to energize and "sermonize" on this issue. Maybe it's just a function of advanced age, or maybe I am too stubborn to continue to look away. But, I will still be a vibrant voice, who reminds you of things you already know, but might not choose to internalize, to actualize. I suggest you change your beliefs about the nature of your life, its meaning and purpose, how you take control of your life, and the choices you make in all of your relationships. But, you must constantly question your motives.

Change is most frightening to people when they lack a firm foundation on which to stand. If they have a strong base of unchanging bedrock values, they are better equipped to weather any storm. That is why the best leadership in times of change is values-based leadership. When both employer and employee know they share a foundation of basic values ... they can move forward together with some measure of confidence despite tremendous change. (Tom Morris)

As T.S. Eliot so compellingly believes, I am repeating the paradoxes of Jesus, of Buddha, of Lao Tzu. *If you would save your life, you must lose it.* Letting go is really the only safe path to embracing change. To that end, it is imperative that we find true meaning in our lives, that *fire within* that brings joy, peace, contentment, spiritual awakening, and growth to all of us. Professor Charles Handy, in his book *The Hungry Spirit* provides four elements necessary to finding that important *meaning* in our lives:

The FIRST, the elusive question of where we are heading, of what success might mean. Nietzsche said that those who have a "why" can endure any "how," but it is the "why" that is difficult. We all need a "telos," a dream of what might be, to give us energy for the journey.

The SECOND, there is the paradoxical doctrine of "Enough." You cannot move on to a different track unless you realize that you have gone far enough on the present one. If you don't know what enough is, in material or achievement terms, you are trapped in a rut of your own devising and will never learn what might be outside that rut.

The THIRD, we all need a taste of the sublime, to lift our hearts, to give us a hint of something bigger than ourselves and of the infinite possibilities of life. The Department. of Education in Britain sums it up rather well, in their official definition of spirituality: "The valuing of the non-material aspects of life, and intimations of an enduring reality."

The FOURTH, and lastly, there is the challenge of immortality. No, we can't live forever, at least in this world, and we can't take anything with us, but we can leave a bit of ourselves behind us, as proof that we made a difference, to someone. That only happens, I believe, by concentrating on others, the ultimate paradox of proper selfishness.

I agree with Dr. Handy that interconnecting these four elements provides meaning, a reason, a purpose for living, even though we cannot predict when one's life ends, or how it ends. For it is truly how life is lived, the journey in life, its challenges, its joy, its disappointments; not the arrival, nor the ending that matters. It is also quite clear to me that these elements relate to both organizations and individuals. But they *ALL* have to do with relationships, which is the most important aspect and dimension of the human experience. But, living is tough. It's difficult and serious business. My friends, it is meant to be that way.

The things that really give meaning to life are the things that are good in themselves, not the means to something else, but the things that are intrinsically good. Those can be very simple things, like helping the needy, enjoying fellowship, and sharing a common meal. We just enjoy being together: we enjoy the food, and we enjoy the company. Today, there is a great hunger for connecting with community in our lives. And, to that end, I think the deepest level of things that are good in themselves inevitably moves toward the direction of religion, a faith, a trust in a higher reality, in the shared fellowship of worship and prayer, where we find the deepest meaning of our lives.

> *Understanding is the reward of faith. Therefore, seek not to understand that you may believe, but believe that you may understand.*
> (St. Augustine)

I think most would agree that religion is not the only place where we find meaning in our lives. Wherever we find activities that are deeply and intrinsically valuable, not as a means, not to prove something, not to show that we're better than someone else, but just good and decent in themselves, such as serving others. At that point, we're close to the core of what the meaning and purpose of life is about.

But given the stress and pressures of just living today, it can be difficult, a bit challenging. Thus, we must learn to live with virtual chaos, ambiguity, confusion, and uncertainty, and not look for certainty, when it is just not going to be available. We are experiencing an explosion of information, literally an information "overload." And this overload is not static. It will increase in speed and intensity. Thus, how do we deal with this, if we remain out of alignment (misalignment)? I submit, it will be with great difficulty. When one experiences confusion, while potentially painful, one realizes that he or she must change the paradigm.

I hasten to add, and I readily admit, that the contents of my book do not speak to the way it is. The contents speak to the way I see it. However, after seriously researching and studying these issues for the past decade, I am convinced that one cannot coast or rely on the knowledge base one has acquired thus far in life. Organizations that are truly pursuing and acquiring excellence are led, not by the "learned," for they live in a world, in a community, that no longer exists, but by curious, *centered,* lifelong learners, passionately committed to imaginative thinking and creativity. Thus, what is one to do? You must truly believe, actualize, and internalize that everything you do daily should contribute to giving your life its relevance, its joy, its true purpose. *If it does not, then don't do it.* Someone once said, "If you're not having fun, you're probably doing something wrong." Everyday of my life, that belief becomes clearer.

> *The best climber in the world is the one who's having the most fun.*
> (Alex Lowe)

Yes, I think we must redefine the word—"work." We should look deep within our core being to focus on what gives our life its true meaning, what we have passion for. Once we discover this sense of spirituality and alignment, you will never "work" again. For who you are and what you are, are more important than what you know. Robert Byron stated, "I believe the purpose of life ... is to live a life with purpose." Well, I believe the purpose of "work" is more than just providing your services for some type of compensation. The purpose of the "work" should be in alignment with how we define our existence, and how we choose to live out our lives.

Les Brown, the popular motivational speaker and successful author, shares the anecdote of someone jumping into their car in a hurry, starting the engine, putting it in gear, and attempting to take off quickly. And, rather than accelerating, with the engine racing, the car groans and starts shaking and vibrating. For a moment, you can't figure out what the heck is going on, until you notice the emergency brake is still on. You quickly pull the release handle, and with the engine racing, the car lunges forward, and accelerates rapidly, hopefully not running into anything. My friends, many people—if not most—go through life with their emergency brakes on. Choose not to.

I loved that movie—*City Slickers*—with Jack Palance and Billy Crystal, especially that casual, very peaceful scene of Jack and Billy riding their horses, discussing what the most important thing in one's life is. Jack said, "It's just one thing." Billy said, "Well, what's the one thing?" Jack held up his index finger. Billy said; "Your finger?" "No, just one thing." Billy incredulously asked "Well, what's the one thing?" Jack replied, "That's for you to figure out." "Once you figure that out, everything else don't mean s - - - ."

As you're the only one you can really change, the only one who can really use all your good advice is yourself. (John-Roger and Peter McWilliams)

This search for self-understanding and meaning in our lives, knowing what really matters, cannot be underestimated, and, once we discover that "one thing," our lives change. Suddenly, our paradigm changes. A whole new world opens up for us. The terrain changes. Your priorities change, both personal and professional. Suddenly, relationships become exceedingly important in your life, all relationships, from a true acceptance of your mortality, to what destiny you choose, to what legacy you will leave your children and your loved ones. Are you on the right career path? Are you emotionally and spiritually mature, committing your life interdependently to advancing the larger community? Are you around people who believe in you, trust you, love you, care about you, not solely as a worker, homemaker, homeprovider, employee, but people who care for you because of what and who you are, not what you know, or how much wealth you have accrued?

Give some thought to the following questions. Carefully, even slowly, read these words. Let me sink in, being mindful of the "one thing" that Jack Palance was referring to.

- Really, who are you?
- What is your life about?
- What is your life mission?
- Where are you headed?
- What is missing in your life?
- Do you love your life thus far?
- Do you live a life of hope or of fear?
- Do you fear what the future holds for you?
- What are your near-term and long-term goals?
- What are the things in your life you most desire?
- If you receive those, how will this change your life?
- What things in your life do you value most?
- What are your most important values and principles?
- What are the various roles that drive your life?
- How are you doing with living a value—and principle-based life?
- Do you live everyday to its fullest as you pursue greatness?
- What would an extraordinarily self-fulfilled life mean to you?
- How do you want to be remembered?

Think about, process, and answer those questions—carefully. Sit down; make a list of the ten most important things in your life. Then, prioritize the list. I have given workshops all over the world, in many cultures, and I have yet to have any participant give me one thing that did not have to do with relationships; starting with the importance you place on yourself, your faith, your freedom, your health, and your loved ones. Professor Charles Handy, of the London School of Economics, has written about satisfying the *hungry spirit,* understanding and internalizing the power of service to others. I suggest it is impossible to extinguish the human spirit.

We must sublimate and subordinate ourselves to advance the larger community, the greater good. And I remind the reader that, as Erich Fromm put it so bluntly, it is "not he who has much that is rich ... but he who gives much." And, to that end, we're going to need a new sense of shared destiny, for we're in this together.

It is strongly suggested that success in today's workplace has never been more tenuous. It's tenuous because the covenant has been broken. Most of us grew up believing if we worked hard, if we were conscientious, we would be taken care of; if we worked hard, we would always have a payday. That's history. Today, working is not good enough. We must work (and I hate that word "work") differently, through different "filters," through different perspectives; one that, in my opinion, reflects the understanding and acceptance that we really never "work" for anyone, but ourselves. Another way to describe what is occurring in today's workplace is to answer the question "are you building a legacy or living from a legacy?"

What we need to do, as individual contributors, as citizens, and as a workforce, is to put less emphasis on just being "employed" and begin to focus on the power and strength of being "employable." The key to our continued employability is to pursue and embrace life's transitions. This is a psychological challenge. When we overcome that obstacle, we can then embrace change, which is physical. While it seems virtually everyone believes in change, very few of us are into "changing." We want the other guy to change.

Surely everyone reading this sentence knows this to be true. But we quite often just choose not to behave this way. I'm reminded of the powerful insight, shared by Schopenhauer, *"Thus, the task is not so much to see what no one yet has seen, but to think what nobody yet has thought about that which everybody sees."*

Now, having shared with you what I truly believe to be the foundational, fundamental anchors of alignment in our lives, I learned a long time ago—and I have been a university professor for some 17 years—that nobody has ever taught anything to anybody. I could be the wisest man in the world and tell you all that I know, but if you don't want to know it, you will not not learn it. It's almost an accident when we learn from being told. I am speaking about the real act of discovery, for as Marcel Proust has described it, it "consists not in finding new lands.... But, in seeing with new eyes."

Once we stop treating organizations and people as machines, and stop trying to re-engineer them, once we move into the paradigm of living systems, organizational change is not a problem. (Margaret Wheatley)

In the 1985 movie, *Dead Poets Society*, Robin Williams portrayed John Keating, an English teacher in an exclusive boy's boarding school. He inspired his students by reciting poetry. One poem in particular, by Walt Whitman, really touched the young men. *Oh Me Oh Life of the questions of these recurring; of the endless strains of the faithless; of cities filled with the foolish. What good amid these Oh Me Oh Life?* Mr. Keating, in a very poignant and moving moment, shared, "Answer—that you are here; that life exists and identity; that the powerful play goes on and you may contribute a verse. What will your verse be?"

So, what will your verse be? What is your destiny, your legacy, your future? Can you create this for yourself? I believe you can. The human capacity to invent and create is universal. Commit yourself to a fidelity of a worthy purpose. Build your life based on what gives it meaning. Look within your heart, for that is where you will find the truth. It is not to be created, but discovered, and acted upon. As I noted in my Introduction, if you don't get this *first Principle* down rather well, you might as well forget about moving on to the other seven. For it is the *mother of all principles*. This one is fundamental—truly foundational—that everything else builds upon. The following words capture so powerfully the theme of this chapter, my first Principle:

I know this now. Every man gives his life for what he believes. Every woman gives her life for what she believes. Sometimes people believe in little or nothing, yet they give their lives to that little or nothing. One life is all we have and we live it as we believe in living it. And then it is gone. But to sacrifice what you are and live without belief, that's more terrible than dying. (Joan of Arc)

Now that we've explored and examined the importance of discovering life's true meaning in our lives, let's do a little self-evaluation. *How would you score yourself on a scale of 1-10,* one representing very little self-knowledge, virtually no self-awareness of what your life is about? Scoring yourself the maximum, a 10, would be the highest rating you could give yourself; a judgement that your life is presently in true alignment with your *life mission statement,* an exciting journey, thus experiencing the true miracle of discovery. Look deeply within your soul; talk to your loved ones; discuss with those who know you the best. Would they agree with your personal assessment of how you view your life and where you derive its true meaning? Is your life one of total *openness*, or one of scheming; one of *true fulfillment*, or one of exploitation and manipulation; one of *deep caring for yourself and others*; or one of loneliness, even quiet desperation? What score would you honestly give yourself?

Now, let me invite you to explore chapter 2, my *principle #2, finding that one thing you love to do ... so you don't have to work again.* Where do you presently stand in this area? Are you absolutely and consistently enthusiastic about how and why you provide your services, your gifts, your talents? Is your *commitment* one of sincere stewardship, or one of *compliance* with someone or something that is controlling, that is more powerful than you? You must know that *complying with...* is *not being fully committed,* where you take ownership of your life, of its processes, of its growth. Thus, let's take a quick quiz. On a scale of 1—10, where do you rank yourself? Giving yourself a grade of 1 or 2 should certainly tell you that a *mid-course correction* is in order. If you grade at about a 9 or 10, which, according to current literature, is exceedingly rare today, you are to be applauded/praised, for you clearly have discovered your passion, your love, your *center*. But, my suspicion is, your score falls somewhere between 4 and 8, and can be improved.

Thus, now, that you have mastered my *principle #1*, that *mother of all principles*, discovering what your life is about, let me encourage you to review and consider my *principle #2*. Odds are that the vast majority of my readers are either keenly aware of, or unwittingly, in psychological transition, believing that their best days, their best, most significant contributions, are still ahead of them. My *principle #2 will help you achieve your dreams.* Enjoy.

2

FIND SOMETHING YOU LOVE TO DO
AND YOU WILL NEVER WORK AGAIN

To love is the only excuse for living.

— Erich Fromm

Between my junior and senior year at the University of Houston, I had to earn sufficient money to pay my tuition for my senior year. In those days, 1963, very few of my friends had the benefit of financial aid, and certainly I didn't. And unable to run the hundred-yard dash in 10 seconds, or leap over tall buildings in a single bound as an athlete, I, along with my friends, had to "work" to pay my way through college. We worked after school, weekends, whatever it took, to get by, doing whatever it took to survive the rigors of academia and to sustain ourselves until we experienced that glorious day—graduation. That was our ticket to leave behind us the pressures of final exams, "all nighters," research papers, pop quizzes, and eight-o'-clock classes.

That summer, I was fortunate enough to land a full-time position, essentially 12 hours per day, six days a week, working for an oil and gas pipeline firm. Now many of you reading this book may know what a "roughnecker" is. But, if you don't, it's a laborer in the oilfields. Well, that summer, between my junior and senior year at the University of Houston, I was a "roughnecker's helper." That's a helper to a laborer, someone who does basically what they are told to do. In fact, they are not paid to think. They are essentially told what to think. They are supposed to leave their brains at home. And, needless to say, there is quite a bit of heavy lifting and outdoor work.

Now, living in north Houston, I had to rely on a Pioneer bus ride early every morning to get me to the boss's house at six a.m. If I recall, riding on that old unairconditioned Pioneer bus, was quite an adventure. But it was pretty economical to ride on them. I think the fare was only a dime. Then we drove to the job site, normally an hour to an hour and a half away, if I recall, somewhere near Kemah, Texas. That summer in Houston, and, if you are familiar with Houston, Texas, in the summer there is really only one temperature, hot and hotter. That summer in Houston, it was an unusually hot season. And, in the oil and gas fields, with virtually no shade, it was common for the temperatures to reach well over 100 degrees. Touching metal in that blazing sun was like touching an open flame. We carried our food and water on our backs, and were fortunate to have, somewhere in the vicinity of the job site, an outdoor "porta john" which came in handy on occasion. My day ended when I arrived back home, normally around 9:00 p.m. I would eat a late snack that my mother had left on the dining room table, take a quick bath, then drag my sore bones to bed. Even though I had quickly figured out this cycle of pain was not what my body could withstand for too many months, I hung in there.

Now, at the end of that summer, while I had probably lost about fifteen pounds, I was successful in saving most of the money I needed to pay my tuition bills, so I had accomplished my main objective. The additional tuition money I required came from a Rotary International College Loan, which my father's boss at Gulf Coast Portland Cement Company was able to get for me. As an aside, even though my salary as a rather junior Air Force officer wasn't that high, I paid back every penny of that loan (some $2,600) within three years of my graduation from the University.

But, after experiencing that dreaded summer, I truly had an epiphany. *I said to myself, "Self, I don't think I want to work anymore." If you want to work, go for it. I think I'll pass. I haven't worked since then.* I realized that there was another way to live one's life, and I chose to take control of my life and truly create my own destiny. For some time, I had thought about military service, and I had concluded that staying in Houston after graduation was just not in my plans. For whatever reason, I'm not really sure, I considered only the Air Force. In fact, my worst fear, was that I was not going to be good enough and meet their high standards, their requirements. To that end, I never even considering talking to the other military service recruiters.

Prior to graduation from college, and I am not seeking sympathy, I was terribly insecure and painfully shy, although I had purposely thrown myself into leadership positions in high school and in college. I even became the Drum Major in my high school band, hoping that this role position would give me the emotional strength to overcome this personality deficiency. I became an officer in my social fraternity, but the fear of public speaking, the pain, was still there. I remained emotionally incapable of standing in front of an audience; standing in front of a room full of people, staring at me, waiting for me to talk to them. I can recall, like it was this morning, being an eighth grader, standing ... in front of a classroom; literally, catatonic, then a sickening feeling in the pit of my stomach and an inability to speak a word. So, with the kids laughing, I walked quickly out of the room, tears running down my cheeks, and into the nearest bathroom, to throw up. I would go home, alone with my thoughts, and feeling ashamed of what I had done. It became so bad, I would become sick just thinking about that moment. In high school, my shyness never really improved. I would practice and practice for hours giving a speech, even with my hands shaking. Then when the moment came, I would make excuses, become ill, do whatever it took, to get out of standing in front of an audience.

So, what could I do? How could I overcome this fear, this shame? I had a choice. I could remain unable to speak in front of an audience, or I could overcome this fear, but how? There was one organization that I knew would provide the leadership skills that I so desperately hungered for. And, my dream, after becoming the first in my family to graduate from college, was to become an officer in the United States Air Force. I just figured, if I could make this happen, it wouldn't get any better than that. And, wow, was I ever right. But, one thing was between me and my Air Force career. To attend Officer Training School (OTS), I had to satisfy all of the degree requirements at the University of Houston.

It's better to be prepared and not have an opportunity—than to have an opportunity and not be prepared. (Whitney Young)

So, at the beginning of my senior year at the University of Houston, I visited the local Air Force recruiter, took a battery of aptitude tests, made arrangements for the necessary flight physical, and told my mom and dad that, if things worked out, I would be attending Officer Training School

(OTS) the following year. My flight physical went fine, except for one little problem. I was 22 years old, loved candy (then), and had never been to a dentist. Consequently, I had a mouth full of bad teeth. The Air Force said I would have to get that situation taken care of by the following May. I said, "no problem," not having a clue as to how I was going to pay a dentist to fix my teeth. The answer was the University of Texas School of Dentistry. I discovered the students would work on me, virtually for free. And, while there were a few interesting moments with the students, on balance, it wasn't too bad. My cavities were taken care of. I signed the required forms that fall, and was "pipe-lined" into an OTS class, conditional upon receiving my degree from the University of Houston in May of 1964. The opportunity of a lifetime was in front of me. My worst fear was that they might change their mind. Fortunately, they didn't. As an aside, regarding my teeth, the Air Force invested considerably in me over my years of active duty, and I was even blessed with much needed braces, and even a few caps. Now I was pumped, primed, and focused on fulfilling my dream. Was I ready for the Air Force? You bet. Was I prepared? You bet. I had found that *fire within.*

> *Not to take possession of your life plan is to let your existence be an accident.* (Irvin D. Yalom)

Was it a tough 90-day Officer Training School? You bet. If it were easy, it wouldn't have been worth anything. But it was worth a great deal. I had discovered a power that had been within me all along. Having graduated from the University of Houston, with degrees in psychology and sociology, I went on to OTS and became a "Ninety-Day Wonder," a freshly minted Second Lieutenant in the United States Air Force. I did have one fairly major obstacle to overcome. The academics, marching, military discipline, and regimentation went pretty well, but toward the end of the 90-day program, I was required to pass a swimming test ... and I didn't know how to swim. If I recall, we had to swim two lengths of a 25-yard pool, but I knew that I could push my body through the distance only *below the surface.* If I swam on top of the water, with my head exposed, after a few seconds, I would very quickly be taking on fairly heavy loads of water. So, I, and one fellow officer trainee, who said he was from inner city Detroit and could not swim, and, like myself, was nervous about this activity, told each other that we were going to somehow do this, or literally drown trying. We discussed our strategy, took deep breaths, shook hands, and went for it. Well, needless to say, we didn't drown, and we both graduated. I still remember the other officer trainees in our class applauding us when we finished this ordeal. The power of the human spirit is truly amazing. I would add, that since then I have learned how to swim well.

Now, I recall vividly my recruiter telling me the prior year that after my commissioning, I "had a lock on Tokyo." I thought, "Wow." I just turned twenty-three years old and I had never been north of Dallas, Texas; what a thrill to be going to Tokyo, Japan for my first tour of duty. Well, surprise, surprise; my orders came in right before OTS graduation: the Air Defense Sector at Sioux City, Iowa. I thought there must be a mistake. There wasn't. So, after a couple of technical training at schools in Florida and Missis-sippi, I arrived in Sioux City and discovered it really wasn't so bad, although that winter was a bit of a challenge. Being from Houston, I had always thought when it got cold, it was cold. Thus, it really couldn't get any colder—than cold; Wrong. That winter, Sioux City experienced a terrible blizzard, and, needless to say, this kid from Texas was ready for a change. It just had to get better. It did.

After about a year in Sioux City, I volunteered for duty in Vietnam. I figured that was where the action was. And, again, a surprise, I was sent to Taiwan for a remote one-year tour. It was a fantastic experience. Following my tour in Taiwan, I had a relatively short period of duty at Richards-Gebaur Air Force Base in Missouri, then on to the Defense Intelligence College, Washington, D.C., for a one-year school tour. That is where my life and my Air Force occupational speciality changed. Prior to graduation, I again volunteered for Vietnam duty and received an assignment to Korat Royal Thai Airbase in Thailand. After completing a six-month Air Combat training class at Cape Cod, Massachusetts, I went on to Air Force Survival School in Washington State, then Jungle Survival Training in the Philip-pines, and then, was extremely privileged to serve a one-year tour of duty, flying 78 combat missions as a Standardization and Evaluation Intelligence Officer on an EC-121R reconnaisance aircraft. Again, it wasn't work. It was a true "love affair," and I enjoyed immensely that experience; and was blessed and grateful to have served my country when asked.

I have chosen to give you, my reader, a little "thumbnail sketch" of my early career in the Air Force, because I think it captures the essence of what I describe as truly finding something you love to do, thus, never having to work anymore. It is how we embrace a paradigm of discovering what life is about and discovering how fulfilling and rewarding it can be. In the *Road Less Traveled*, psychiatrist Dr. M. Scott Peck defines love as "the will to extend one's self for the purpose of nurturing one's own or another's spiritual growth." Or, as Cullen Hightower describes love, it's "what's left in a relationship after all the selfishness has been removed." I don't think I can improve on that insight.

Let me briefly back up just a bit and share with you an incident that occurred at the Air Force Survival School that had such a profound impact on my life. As a volunteer, as were all Air Force personnel during the Vietnam conflict, I was required to attend the very challenging sixteen-day survival course at Fairchild AFB, Wahington State. There were no exceptions to this established, long-standing policy. We were well briefed on what to expect, and were aware that the average weight loss for all students, depending on the season, was somewhere around 15-18 pounds. All Air Force combat aircrew had to attend and had to graduate from this school. There were no exceptions. Basically, what the resident staff did to you there was try to kill you (almost), as you experienced unrelenting discomfort and self-reflection. Now if you "survived" the sixteen days, you would then have the marvelous opportunity to fly air combat missions over Vietnam and Laos, with people shooting real bullets and missiles at you. Was that a good deal ... or what?

Now, was it easy to flunk out of this school? (I'm glad I asked.) All one had to do was just say to the resident staff at the school, at any time during the sixteen days, three little letters, S.I.E., which stood for Self-Initiated Elimination. There would be no questions asked further of you. You would be sent back to your last command, but your Air Force career would undoubtedly be essentially aborted at that point. To my knowledge, we lost no one in my class. All chose to stay, for we knew we were going to experience the most expensive, most rewarding, and important education in our lifetimes.

Well, for some three days of the sixteen, we encountered an adversarial force whose task was to seriously deny us virtually all of life's comforts. As I recall, the students—in isolation and in total darkness, without any contact with other students—were forced to stand straight up in large boxes, and stay there, without touching the sides of the box, without sleep, food, or water, and experience this horrendous music playing continuously at about 120 decibels. The adversary team would watch us and provide creative disincentives if we chose to misbehave or not comply with their orders. And something quite remarkable happened for me during those roughly 72 hours in that box. In my particular box, I discovered a slight crack in the corner, right along my hairline, and I realized I could tiptoe and look outside through the crack. And, as unbelievable as it might sound, I convinced myself that, if I could see or discern the sun coming up, I was going to have a great day, and, during my stay in the box, the sun came up twice. *Now, I have not had a bad day since then. But, I do admit some days are greater than others.* But not bad days, none. In fact, I convinced myself that I had it better than everybody else in the whole world, for I truly loved the Air Force and was even grateful for this challenging program, because I chose to believe I would be a better person, a better officer, for the experience. And I still believe that.

To complete the Air Force Survival School portion of my chapter on *Never Working Again*, on the 16th morning, after I had counted my toes and fingers, it appeared that I was, indeed, going to survive and graduate. Our commencement speaker that morning was a young Air Force Captain, obviously a graduate of the survival school, but one whose F-4E aircraft had been recently shot down near KheSan, in northern South Vietnam. He bailed out and, upon landing, encountered a few of the enemy and was captured by the Vietcong. However, after about three days, he was successful in escaping and evading the enemy, and we were able to effect a rescue. Though a bit shaken up emotionally, he was not injured. The Air Force flew him back to the States, so he could visit his family for a few days, but before returning to the Vietnam theatre, and on his way back, he had been invited to speak to the graduating class of the Air Force Survival School.

The class was excited to hear what he had to say. We knew he was a graduate of the school, and we wanted to know how he had survived, and what he had relied upon to facilitate the rescue. He began by speaking about how his aircraft had adroitly intercepted a surface-to-air missile, his bailing out, and his slow descent to the ground. As he approached the ground, he was quickly surrounded by some Vietcong, who were clearly not friendly. Now, when you fly, you wear a velcro-supported vest over your flight suit. It carries a suppy of local maps, certain letters in the language of the region, money, sugar water, medications of all kinds, a small 38-revolver, certain electronic emitters, a flashlight, and other types of survival gear.

Well, he told us that the first thing the Vietcong did when he landed amongst them, was to remove his vest. Bummer! Here we had experienced literally sixteen days of absolute Hell, to learn how to survive, and the first thing the Vietcong had done was to deny him all the gear that we had to rely upon for our survival. But then he said the following: Gentlemen, what brought him out of the potentially deadly situation of his capture was not his survival vest. It was not what he was carrying on the outside that led to his freedom. It was the inner strength that he was carrying on the inside that brought him freedom, freedom back to the greatest country in the world, America. He spoke eloquently of his love for his country, for the Air Force, and the privilege to serve his President, the Commander-In-Chief. He truly loved what he did. And, I am confident, he did not see himself as just "working."

> *Only to the extent that someone is living out this self transcendence of human existence, is he truly human or does he become his true self. He becomes so, not by concerning himself with his self's actualization, but by forgetting himself and giving himself, over-looking himself and focusing outward.* (Viktor Frankl)

Albert Camus shared this marvelous insight, "What sordid misery there is in the condition of a man who works and in a civilization based on men who work." As pressures rise higher and higher in today's workplace, we are falling victim to feeling that we must do more of the same and do it harder, faster, and longer than ever before. This idea is compounded by the fact that more of us than ever are holding back on our most productive work ethic when we arrive at the workplace. Every day, millions of us feel out of touch with why we're working so much, or even why we are receiving a paycheck. Again, discover what your life is about, what gives it meaning and purpose, *first*. Then, the *doing* is a piece of cake ... or at least three Oreo cookies. And it is my deep belief that you can be whatever you resolve to be.

> *Neither possession, nor power, nor sensuous satisfaction ... can fulfill man's desire for meaning in his life; he remains in all this separate from the whole, hence unhappy. Only in being produc-tively active ... and to experience love ... can man make sense of his life.* (Eric Fromm)

To find meaning in the everyday things, to see the divine in others, to discover holiness in the most mundane of activities, we must understand the power of the spirit of coming together in a commitment to public virtue, the need for community and a deep connection with others. Burnout or "brownout" is not an issue of working too hard; it is a matter of finding no meaning in what we do, essentially, a *crisis of spirit*. It is a lack of emotional energy, rather than a deficit of mental or physical energy.

Most of us still are wandering through life, experiencing various degrees of frustration and disillusionment, with vague goals of pursuing happiness, success, material wealth that are useless at best and laughable at worst. Now there is nothing inherently wrong with achieving these goals but rather than pursuing them, they must be encountered along life's journey, experienced/achieved as "by products" of one's purpose/meaning in life and commitment to serving others, the larger community, the larger good.

> *It's important not to have any specific ambitions or desires. It's more important to have ambitions in terms of the way you want to live your life, and then the other things will flow out of that.* (Derek Bell)

It takes a reasonable dose of courage to overcome one's fear to break free of the chains that hold us back. Courage is the capacity to achieve a higher level of maturity; to go ahead in spite of the fear, or in spite of the pain. Raise that "high bar" every day on your potential for further growth, emotional, intellectual, and spiritual. It's your choice. *Argue for your limitations, and sure enough they are yours* (Richard Bach).

Choose not to be a spectator; choose not to live a life of frustration and quiet desperation. Choose to reach for that higher level of thinking and contributing; choose to discover what you love to do. This will change your paradigm, your map, your terrain, opening a totally new vista of opportunities for further growth. It will be a different life. Choose to invest in relationships. Choose to serve others, lifting the spirits of those whom you come in contact with everyday. Choose to love life. Choose to be enthusiastic about this marvelous gift, and about its vast potential, a gift we call life. Avoid WORK. If you're not having fun, and you're not loving life to its fullest, not loving what you do, what you have passion for, giving of yourself, serving others, then you're probably doing something you shouldn't be doing.

> *We expect to be loved and are quick to condemn those who do not comply. We believe that life comes with a guarantee that we will be loved. It rarely occurs to us that the degree to which we are loved is directly related to our lovability.*

We are all acquainted with individuals who are constantly moody, who look for the dark side of everything, who are fearful of commitment, who shirk from responsibility, who flare up at the least provocation and then wonder why they are not sought after, why they are not loved. Who would love such a person except someone who is asking for unhappiness?

It is when we ask for love LESS and begin giving it MORE that the basis of human love is revealed to us. (Leo Buscaglia)

One of my favorite stories about "jobs" and "work" is that of the four bricklayers who, when asked by a traveler to describe what they were doing, provided four different answers. The first said simply, "I am laying bricks." The second responded, "I am feeding my family by laying bricks." The third said, "I am putting up a wall." The fourth, with a sense of great spirit, said, "I am constructing a cathedral, thereby giving honor and praise to the Lord; a cathedral for people to come and worship." Life's fulfillment comes through our greatest resources—imagination; commitment and creativity; service to a cause, an idea, a mission, or others external to ourselves; and a purpose with a transcendent character. It is the collective and participative imagination that animates organizations, that gives life to them. Choose to be a dreamer; change your paradigm, your map. *Choose, with great passion, your calling in life—and you will never work again.*

I place a great deal of emphasis and importance on this chapter. It speaks to the quest for purpose in our lives. And that purpose and meaning has to be an intention to leave the world a little better than we found it. Our responsibility to others relies on our responsibility to ourselves, a choice to love ourselves and the responsibility to choose our destiny. It begins in the human heart, where the passions of wonder and awe are natural that *"fire within."* And it remains my belief that *the heart of the problem, the heart of misalignment and dysfunction in most organizations (as well as in people today) is a problem of the heart.*

The salvation of the human world lies nowhere else than in the human heart, in the human power to reflect, in human meekness and human responsibility. Without a global resolution in human consciousness, nothing will change for the better and the catastrophe towards which this world is headed will be unavoidable. (Vaclav Havel)

Now that you have finished the chapter, examined this *principle*: How would you rate yourself, on a scale of 1-10, one being *I hate my job*; 10 being *every day is a love affair and every day is a holiday*? Have you chosen to understand the marvelous principle of putting things asked of you first; and things you ask of others and organizations second? Individuals who truly love life, who have discovered that *fire within*, have a powerful *value system based on universal principles of integrity, honor, fairness, justice, and trustworthiness.* You have a *moral compass*; you are *self reliant, have a passion for excellence, possess* a *self-confidence* which you rely upon for *sound judgments*. How did you rate yourself? Be honest. Might there be room for some improvement in this area?

My next *principle,. #3, servant leadership*, speaks about the power of committing ourselves to the larger good, the larger community. On a scale of 1-10, how would you score on that test? Might you score on the low side; are you someone who is selfish, out to enhance your own personal agenda, manipulating and exploiting other people? Or might you score quite high, understanding that it is only through acts of selflessness that you have any chance at all to achieve your highest level of potential? I invite you to read chapter 3 to be provoked and challenged by the power of *principle #3, servant leadership.*

3

EMBRACE SERVANT LEADERSHIP

Ambition is most mature, not when we know what we want and how to get it, but when we understand what we possess, and how to give it.

— Eugene Kennedy

I've often thought of the powerful insight and wisdom of Dag Hammarskjold, who said, "it is more noble to give yourself to one individual than to labor in support of the masses." What was he saying? What was at the core of this belief? I have concluded that those individuals who understand and discover the power of internalizing "servant leadership" to advance the larger good will have successfully pursued and achieved life's fulfillment.

The deepest part of human nature is that which urges people— each one of us—to rise above our present circumstances and to transcend our nature. If you can appeal to it, you tap into a whole new source of human motivation. How do we give "air" and "life" creative power to the human spirit that produces value in individual lives and in organizations? While you may be able to buy someone's hand and back, you cannot buy their heart, mind, and

spirit. Servant Leadership represents the deciding point between an organization's enduring success or its eventual extinction.
(Stephen R. Covey)

I firmly believe that this principle, this concept of servant leadership, is self-affirming, a natural law; and, if truly understood, in all of its power, would be universally accepted. It has been around in recorded history, literally, since earliest man, who lived off the land, who protected the weak, who sacrificed their lives for their brothers, and their hunting band. Their conscious choice was to consistently sublimate and subordinate their personal interests to advance the larger community. They believed that no one person had the answer; we need everyone's creativity to find our way through this crazy world, and the larger group is more important than any individual. And their meaning, their purpose in life, was to serve, contribute, and make a difference. Albert Einstein said, *the highest destiny of the individual is to serve rather than to rule.*

The servant-leader is servant first, beginning with the natural feeling that one wants to serve; then conscious choice brings one to aspire to lead, but not leading without direction. It is important to realize the servant-leader believes in basic human goodness and has both a visionary and implementation role while creating and nurturing processes and organizations that depend on human capacity. Humans desire, and I believe, inherently need to serve each other. For it is through human service to others that we find meaning in our lives.

If you seek enlightenment for yourself simply to enhance yourself and your position, you miss the purpose; if you seek enlightenment for yourself to enable you to serve others, you are with purpose.
(Dali Lama)

I spent twenty-six years in the service of my country as an Air Force officer, and I was grateful for every day of that experience. To serve my country and to be an American, truly, it didn't get much better than that. And I was so fortunate to be around other terrific people who loved their country, strongly, in their duty and their service. I want to share with my readers a little story that exemplifies what I mean by servant leadership. It's an anecdote, an incident that happened while I was serving on the Joint Chiefs of Staff.

As an Air Force Lieutenant Colonel, sometime around the mid-'80's, I was serving my second tour of duty at the Pentagon. I had served previously, as a Captain back in the early '70's, having just returned from an air combat tour in Vietnam. A new, recently promoted, Air Force Officer had been assigned as our Director, Lieutenant General Alfred Hanson. A very impressive gentleman, General Hanson had come to us from the Air Force Staff and was very familiar with the Pentagon's organizational culture we referred to as "Disneyland East." (After flying 78 air combat missions over Vietnam and Laos, I didn't know what real combat was until I began serving my second tour of duty at the Pentagon on the Joint Chiefs of Staff). The Joint Staff, at that time, was seen as a true "meat grinder" of a job; it could really cause "psychological overload," and resulted in the premature retirements of many action officers, especially in the grade of Lieutenant Colonel, which I was at that time. I don't know specifically what the average tenure of a Lieutenant Colonel or Colonel on the Joint Staff was at that time, although I had heard it was some 24 months. As an aside, I served five years on the Joint Chiefs of Staff, and it was truly a most marvelous, educational experience, for I grew everyday.

General Hanson had been with the Joint Staff for about a month and had invited all of the senior officers, their spouses or significant others, over to his home at Bolling AFB for a dinner party. Well, being a Lieutenant Colonel, and after receiving the invitation from a Lieutenant General to join him at his home for dinner, I quickly checked my organizer to see if I could work it into my schedule. (Just kidding. Obviously, I could work it into my schedule). My wife and I attended the party, and very predictably, General Hanson was "Mr. Personality." Marvelous hosts, he and his wife were hugging and kissing everything that was moving, serving the roughly 75 guests.

After all had finished their meals, General Hanson started moving everyone into a large family room, where he wanted to make a few remarks. My blessed wife—one of those individuals rarely impressed with anything, or anyone, at any time—giggled somewhat and said to me, "Look, he is fixing to give a speech." And, he was.

General Hanson first welcomed everyone to his home and said he hoped to have other opportunities where we could enjoy fellowship together. I remember him vividly saying, "I am very happy and privileged to be your Director, and I want you to know you are my first team because, at this Directorate, there is no second team. And I want you to know that I am going to ask you to take some risks; and, occasionally, you are going to get in trouble. But, that's okay because, when you do, I'll get you out of trouble. But I want you to know that I deeply care about everyone of you." He actually used the word "care" and, even my wife didn't snicker because she knew that he truly meant it, not almost meant it. He truly cared about us. (It had always been my belief, as a former air combat guy, that the one correlation between having a military order given, in combat, and it actually being carried out, depended on only one thing, just one thing; namely, did the person giving the order care about you? Did they care about you, not solely as a body, a warrior, an employee, or as a subordinate, but as a person, a human being who was unique and very special)?

This is the essence of servant leadership; and true servant leaders reflect the understanding that servant leadership works only when it is "mutual." *It exists everywhere, or it is nowhere* (Peter Senge). Now, as an aside, General Hanson expected us to work only half the time, but, he didn't care which twelve hours it was. Yes, he was a pretty tough, driven, focused, visionary servant leader, but, we would walk through a wall for that man, or at least try. He subsequently was promoted to full General and retired as the Commanding General of the Air Force Logistics Command.

What I am speaking to is that servant leaders make sure other individuals' highest priority needs are being served. General Hanson's paradigm of leadership was that he served those personnel who reported to him. And, as a true servant leader, General Hanson did not view the staff as working under him, per se; they worked for themselves and had acquired an appetite for both responsibility and accountability. They were committed to advancing the larger good, thus, serving in the defense of the United States of America, but also serving our nation's strategic interests and General Hanson, as well .

> *If you look closely you will see that almost anything that really matters to us, anything that embodies our deepest commitment to the way human life should be lived and cared for ... depends on some form ... often, many forms ... of service to others.* (Margaret Mead)

I hasten to add that servant leadership is not a "quck fix," or a "let's turn it around this weekend" shift in management style. In fact, it has very little to do with management, which has to do with controlling resources (things). It has everything to do with serving others and having visionary leadership, which has everything to do with inspiring human beings to self-motivate, to pursue and acquire greatness in their lives. It reflects a personal transformation which is absolutely essential for organizations to transform themselves. And it takes time, but it is potentially life changing.

What are the characteristics of servant leaders? After studying organizational behavior literature for these past ten years, I have chosen to describe these as stages, steps, or layers ... that are sequential in nature. If you don't get that first one right, you'll never even get close to the next one. Thus, the first and, I believe, the key trait is that the individual must be absolutely committed to advancing the "larger good"; i.e., a larger, more important journey than their personal pursuit of happiness. This is the critical quality, without which, they will never approach the next phase. Thus, *principles #1, #2 and #3 are absolutely vital qualities/traits/accomplishments if you have any chance at all for greatness.* These are foundational in nature, upon which the other five principles rest. And, as a brief reminder—just saying you are committed to advancing the larger good is not the same as advancing the larger good. We all should know or be familiar with the wisdom, the axiom shared by Margaret Thatcher, *No one would remember the Good Samaritan if he had only good intentions.* One must act!

Mohandas K. Gandhi was a short, thin, ailing, ugly, and frightened child, afraid especially of snakes, ghosts, and the dark. In school, he was painfully average and painfully shy, not even desiring to talk to anyone. Yet, as he grew spiritually, he began to understand the power of servant leadership, dedicating his life to a larger good. He became one of the most inspiring figures of our time when he led the Indian struggle for independence and countless other nonviolent struggles of the past century.

I have nothing new to teach the world. Truth is as old as the hills.
(Gandhi)

Gandhi's principles of truth and service to others are exemplified by the following legacies:

- His strong belief that all people can shape and guide their lives according to the highest ideals.
- His strong opposition to social, ethnic, and religious intolerance.
- His insistence that personal change and the ability to bring about social change through service to others are linked.

And how did he put these principles to test? During the struggle for Indian independence from the England, members of Parliament, who had heard about this powerful Gandhi, invited him to come to Parliament, to England, to speak before them. He accepted their invitation. On that given day, at the appointed time, with Parliament seated, they waited to view this powerful individual they had heard so much about. So into the chambers walked Gandhi, surrounded by his close aides and advisors. They were absolutely stunned. He must not have weighed more than 80 pounds, wrapped in some type of a loin cloth, and barefoot. They didn't know whether to laugh or cry.

Because of his sight build, some of the clerks in the Hall of Parliament had to find a small stool for Gandhi to stand on at the podium. Then, when things quieted down, he began to talk. Slowly at first, almost methodically, his tempo and rhythm quickened; then, he hit his pace. Gandhi spoke compellingly, powerfully, for almost two hours. He spoke without notes, without any assistance of a prepared statement. When he finished, the members of Parliament gave him a huge round of applause. The applause continued for two full minutes. They were, needless to say, impressed with this Gandhi.

He acknowledged their applause and appreciation for his presentation; then, very soberly, he stepped down from his stool, and started to walk away. At that moment, members of the English press rushed to him, to inquire as to how he could have spoken for nearly two hours without any notes to such a gathering of prominent legislators. Having difficulty getting through the ring of advisors and aides, they inquired how could Gandhi do this? One could easily surmise that most outside speakers would find such a gathering intimidating. One of his close advisors said, "You have to understand Gandhi. What he says he believes and what he believes, he does." For it, indeed, was Gandhi's belief that "life is one inextricable whole; thus, one cannot do right in one department of life whilst he is occupied in doing wrong in another."

What is Freedom? It is the total absence of concern for yourself. And the best way to quit being concerned with yourself is to be concerned about ... and to serve others. (Florinda Donner)

My research into "management" and servant leadership goes back some two decades. Most of the people, today, who have a title of "manager," might manage themselves reasonably well, but they rarely contribute any value to their organizations. In fact, I have observed that most do more harm than good. This "layered" model, reflecting a "power over or control over" approach to organizational structures goes back literally hundreds, if not thousands, of years, essentially coming out of the Middle Ages, the church, and the military. And, unfortunately, this structure still exists in some "sick" organizations today. It stems from a perverted opinion that people are things. It's my belief that people do not want to be managed, nor do they need to be managed. It remains my view that they need psychological air, allowing them freedom to pursue their dreams, while they commit themselves to a high level of integrity, nurturing an appetite of self-responsibity and self-accountability; and, at the same time, demanding that all in the organization embrace this paradigm as well.

In organizations that are truly committed to excellence, this "management" paradigm of "control over" ... and lack of trust has been thrown into the "dust pans of history." I am NOT suggesting that we do not require *checks and balances*. I am NOT suggesting that we should be reckless with judgments, certainly decisions that affect the judicious use of resources. I am suggesting that an optimum culture is one that is both *loose and tight* simultaneously. This is no longer just organizational theory. It is effectively practiced in many organizations today that are truly committed to excellence.

It was Robert Greenleaf, the visionary leader of American Telephone and Telegraph Corporation for so many years who stated, "Servant leadership begins with the feeling that one wants to serve first. Then conscious chice brings one to aspire to lead. The difference manifests itself in the care taken by the servant to make sure that other people's highest priority needs are being served. The best test is this: Do those served grow as persons; do they, while being served, become healthier, wiser, freer, more autonomous, more likely themselves to become servants?"

The idea of servant is deep in our Judeo-Christian heritage. Servant (along with serve and service) appears in the Bible more than thirteen hundred times. Part of the human dilemma is that the meaning of serve, in practical behavioral terms for both persons and institutions, is never completely clear. Thus one who would be servant is a life-long seeker, groping for light but never finding ultimate clarity. One constantly probes and listens, both to the promptings from one's own inner resources and to the communications of those who are also seeking. Then one cautiously experi-

ments, questions, and listens again. Thus the servant-leader is
constantly growing in self-assurance through experience, but never
having the solace of certainty. (Robert K. Greenleaf)

I was so fortunate, while serving in the Air Force, to see servant leadership in action. I suspect a lot of my readers would question my judgment and observational skills, but, as Peter Senge stated at a Conference I attended a few years ago, "People who have served in military combat know more than anyone about servant leadership." According to many studies carried out by the military, there is only one correlation that inspires men in combat to consistently carry out orders. That is, do they believe their Commanders care about them, not solely as warriors, but as human beings, and would they ask those men in their command to do something that they would choose not to do? I have studied the great field, naval and air commanders, from Napoleon, to Washington, Lee, Jackson, Hancock, Chamberlain, Mosby, MacArthur, LeMay, Halsey, Eisenhower, and Schwarzkopf. And there is consistently one common thread. These great commanders of men were not only very courageous, daring, imaginative, and fearless, but were also men of great character. They cared deeply for the men in their command, and they showed it.

Character formation lays the psychic foundation for the ability
both to mobilize to a task and to behave morally by being able to
control impulses and defer gratification. (Amitai Etzioni)

So, what character traits do effective servant leaders display? I offer the following:

- They choose to be powerful, empathic listeners; they listen not solely with the ears, but with the eyes and heart as well.

- They extend themselves and connect with those around them, and certainly with those who look to them for visionary leadership. Like Gandhi, Mother Teresa, and Dr. Martin Luther King, Jr., they nurture this "zone of peace" around themselves that draws others into their presence and circle of influence.

- While they know that the human experience is not about perfection, they are inclined to be extremely trustworthy and honest, honest with themselves and demanding of honesty from those around them. They choose to trust unconditionally, knowing that we all make mistakes. But they know when people make mistakes, they need encouragement and confidence building, not discipline.

- They are terrific stewards ... holding something in trust for another, for a greater good. They are aware of what life's purpose and meaning are truly about, and would agree with Dean Berry, an American writer, who says, "If we are to feel spiritually rewarded, we cannot allow our lives to continue to be compartmentalized, divided, or labelled."

- They have keen intuitive skills and are able to make sound judgments without relying on more and more data to justify their decisions.

- They have foundational, fundamental servant leadership competencies: self-awareness, self-management, social awareness, marvelous intrerpersonal skills, and an amazing capacity to draw others into their zone of peace/influence.

- They have keen neuro-linguistic skills, are immensely talented in reading body language, choosing to be careful with words, and understanding that the "small things" in relationships are "huge."

- While extremely passionate about their lives and what they believe in, they are humble individuals and are comfortable within their skin, very much at peace with themselves.

- They are clearly in alignment regarding personal values and principles. They have high standards of propriety and ethical behavior for themselves and demand it of those around them.

- They reject the cult of self-realization and the pursuit of individual happiness, embracing communal responsibility and accountability.

- They are prone to defend people not in their presence and are not inclined to blame others for personal misjudgments. They have a tendency to say, "Well, that one didn't work out so well. We'll get them next time." They have an appetite for taking sole responsibility for their decisions and desire to be held personally accountable for those judgements.

- They desire to enhance the growth of others around them. Thus, while they may enjoy "constructive verbal conflict," they are deeply respectful of "differences" in all people, all perspectives, faiths, religions, and cultures.

- They believe that individualism has become too isolating and so they rely on the strength of interdependence, and the hero status of "teams." De Tocqueville, looking at America a century and a half ago, was worried about individualism which, he said, "at first, only saps the virtues of public life, but in the long run attacks and destroys all others and is at length absorbed in downright selfishness."

- They believe that all people have intrinsic value beyond their tangible contributions as employees. As such, they deeply believe in nurturing the spiritual, personal, and professional growth of people.

- They think strategically, always focusing on the larger good, subordinating and sublimating their personal agenda to advance the greater community; and they believe that organizations, certainly businesses, are communities, not properties.

- They focus less on an organization's vision or mission statements and more on engaging conversations about what is possible and how much we care.

- They reflect that "fire within" and consistently lift the spirits of those around them. People feel good about being in their presence. They are extremely trustworthy and demand trustworthiness from those around them, believing that "self leadership" is the essence of initiative. David Whyte speaks to this power in one of his poems: "Always this energy smoulders inside ... when it remains unlit ... the body fills with dense smoke."

- They stretch themselves, welcome surprises, and encourage those around them to reach their highest levels of performance, often expecting more than that person believes he or she can accomplish. They believe strongly in team synergy.

- They are typically of deep faith.

To whom much has been given, much will be demanded; and from the one who has been entrusted with much, much more will be asked. (Luke 12:48)

Choose not to pursue happiness or success for yourself, for it will always elude you. However, if you choose to seek happiness and success for others, more often than not, you will find it. In fact, you should choose not to pursue success at all. Rather, you encounter it along life's journey. The key to true servant leadership is really quite simple. You commit yourself to advancing the larger community, the larger good. You have a clear vision of what your life is about, what direction you are moving in. You live life to the fullest, identifying a path which reflects a personal alignment of values and principles. You give power away, not unlike love; you genuinely trust people; you believe deeply in the value and potential of all people; and you model behavior. And *you walk humbly with your God* (Book of *Micah*, 6:8).

Service is the virtue that distinguishes the great of all times and which they will be remembered by. It places a mark of nobility upon its disciples. It is the dividing line which separates the two great groups of the world—those who help and those who hinder, those who lift and those who lean, those who contribute and those who only consume. How much better it is to give than to receive. Service in any form is comely and beautiful. To give encouragement, to impart sympathy, to show interest, to banish fear, to build self-confidence and awaken hope in the hearts of others; in short—to love them and to show it—is to render the most precious service. (Bryant S. Hinckley)

Now, let's take a short quiz. On a scale of 1-10, how would you score on exercising consistently *servant leadership*? If you judge yourself on the low end, there is a lot of personal change and transformation that must be accomplished. Or, you can just choose to rely on past successes for future success, which is clearly problematic today. If you judge yourself to be on the high end, that is, an 8 or above, you are on your way to true greatness. You probably know that already.

My next chapter, *principle #4,* captures the essence of achieving true effectiveness by *freely giving power away.* Before you study this *principle,* how would you rate yourself on a scale of 1-10? Might your perspective, your paradigm, be out of alignment? I invite you to review my *principle #4 on what truly constitutes power, both individual and organizational.* I do suggest that you open your mind, embrace your vulnerabilities and self-doubt; unclog those filters that inhibit true growth. Enjoy.

4

FREELY GIVE POWER AWAY

He that hath no rule over his own spirit is like a city that is broken down and without walls.

— Proverbs 25:28

Let me please start this chapter out with a little anecdote of the fascinating dynamics of an incident that happened at a fast-food restaurant; then, I will suggest a clear connection to this incident exists to one's personal life, the choices we choose to make, and the ethical use of power.

About three years ago, when I was about to leave the Shenandoah University campus, my wife called me and asked that I drop by Roy Roger's Restaurant on the way home and pick up an 8-piece ... box of fried chicken for my family. Now, I don't normally eat fried chicken, but, as a dutiful husband, when my spouse asks me to pick up something on the way home, like a laser beam, I'm looking for it to bring it home to my family.

Arriving at the drive-through, fast-food restaurant, I got in line and placed my order, only to be rewarded by a voice that advised, "We are temporarily out of fried chicken. You will have to come back in about 25 minutes." After pausing and reflecting for a moment, I shared with the friendly voice on the "squawk box" that this was hard to believe. It was 5:30 in the afternoon, and, after all, this was Roy Roger's. They never run out of fried chicken. She said, "I'm sorry, but you will have to come back in a few minutes." I said I couldn't come back in a few minutes. Being the brilliant gum-chewing intellect, I asked her, very respectfully, to please walk over to that large aluminum food tray some 15 feet behind her and check just one more time. "I just feel that you have overlooked something or have been misinformed, I said, "there just has to be a supply of fried chicken over there." After an apparent, awkward, momentary hesitation, she agreed.

Some 15 seconds later, she returned and said, "Okay, we unfortunately are temporarily out of breast meat, white meat, but we've got six pieces." Without hesitation, I said, "I'll take what you've got." Upon reaching the pickup window, that rectangular shape opening that provides some 75% of America's nourishment and nutrition, I said quite respectfully, "You know I've been thinking. You really want me to be an exceedingly happy customer when I leave here in a moment, right?" The nice lady hesitated briefly, then with somewhat of a nervous response, said, "Sure." Then, why don't you just throw in a quart of coleslaw?" She said, "What? I can't throw in a quart of coleslaw." I told her I really wanted an 8-piece box of fried chicken, which would have included some white meat, which she didn't have, so perhaps she could could just throw in a quart of coleslaw. "You can do it. You have my permission," I said.

Exasperated, the nice "window woman" said, "Sir, I don't make the rules here. I can sell you a quart of cole slaw. I cannot just throw it in. I said, "Sure you can. You own this place." She said, "Sir, I only sell fried chicken here."

Observing her obvious frustration and haste to get me off the property as quickly as she could, the on-duty manager was standing some 6 feet behind her, undoubtedly monitoring our conversation, but apparently not wanting any part of it. I knew she was the manager. She was wearing a different colored shirt, a bit of a weird practice, don't you think? The manager leans over and handed a quart of coleslaw to her and, somewhat reluctantly, said, "Give this to him."

Now, it is not my intention to disparage, blame, or be critical, in any way, of the nice woman at the window. She was a delightful person who was doing what she had been scripted to do, adhering to some policy. I strongly fault the management that created and nurtured a culture that would deny this lady the freedom to make individual choices, freedom to make reasonable choices without fear of retribution or punishment. And you must know that in order not to just prosper today in business, but to survive, you don't just satisfy the external customer. *You must WOW the customer today. If you choose not to, you will go out of business. (WOW-ING the customer occurs when after the transaction the external customer leaves, saying WOW, a very enthusiastic and positive WOW.) If this happens, and happens consistently, there is a chance, no guarantees, but a chance, your business will be successful. If you don't see or hear BIG WOWS, the chances of you remaining in business, certainly in America, are problematic.*

At this point, the most important, and likely the least compensated, person at this Roy Rogers Restaurant, the "window woman," was relieved that it appeared I would soon be out of there. I thanked her and told her, "You don't just sell fried chicken. Don't ever say that. You own this place. You are Roy Rogers. You are its Ambassador. You are the Chairman of the Board of Directors of their parent organization. You are by far the key stakeholder in this entire enterprise, and you must know that it's always easier to get forgiveness than permission." One can only imagine what she thought of this little speechette. She blinked a few times and said, "Bye."

So, what's the moral of the story? If you truly aspire to greatness in your life, you must take genuine ownership of the journey you're on; and in an organizational context, it's a collective journey. In the service business today, and the vast majority of positions today, certainly those created in the last decade, are in the service sector, the companies that are truly acquiring excellence, don't just sell or transact the selling of products and services. They create a positive, emotional experience for their external customers. They connect, and in a significant way, create a brief relationship with their customers. And, in those organizations, the senior, more visible, influential leaders in that organization know to treat all employees and encourage each to treat each other in a way, that you want your very best external customers treated. *Indeed, I would suggest, that the most important customer is the internal customer, your co-workers and peers, not the external customer that ultimately buys your products or services.*

One of the more important tasks of all of us, irrespective of official duties, is to create imaginative and participative conversations that bring out the best in ourselves and others. Now, it is not unreasonable that we have "big L leaders and little L leaders" but all are leaders. And tomorrow's leaders will value and be more loyal to principles than they value their companies, or organizations; thus creating the conditions where human ingenuity can flourish. Margaret Wheatley has recently and quite accurately stated that, *"Western culture, for some three centuries, has nurtured a belief that machines, providing dominion and control, can install new attitudes, re-engineer organizations, and provide increased efficiencies. For every problem, we relied upon technical solutions, even if technology was the cause of the initial problem."* This hypnotic, seductive, image of power reflects a confusion of the machine metaphor with reality, where historically we have believed life was a machine. It's my view, with respect to organizational performance, efficiency, and effectiveness, that we have historically attempted to control that which we feared. Continuing to deny the existence of human spirit, will, passion, and compassion (the *fire within)* keeps us away from the operative paradigm in organizations truly committed to excellence.

Most individuals are far more capable of greater productivity than their present jobs require, or even expect. But senior management (leaders) in most organizations still don't believe it. The language of "empowerment" is introduced, but the "tired" style/model of benevolent-authoritarian management rarely changes. Traditionally, we have defined "power" as a constraint on open discussion, which potentially has undermined the critical dimension of dialogue. Real empowerment, and not just "cosmetic" improvement, is not something that is provided on loan. *People who really understand power give it away ... and, not unlike love, the more you give away, the more it returns to you.* Unfortunately, many managers assume there is a limited supply of power, that giving power to another means diminishing one's own power. This is wrong. People who are truly "powerful"—and I am NOT referring to people in positions of authority; I am talking about influence—understand that using power ethically, and in a principle-based manner, liberates and frees individuals. It gives them "psychological" air, making them more innovative, imaginative, and dramatically enhances the potential of conversation, which leads us to insights and critical self-reflection through experiencing and truly connecting with each other. The good leader causes you to have confidence in them. The great leader, who truly understands the ethical use of power, causes you to have confidence in yourself.

The fundamental issue remains that it is absolute folly to recognize the complexity of human life and attempt to organize it away. And it is ludicrous to continue to believe that people are most strongly motivated by promises of personal gain, rather than by our powerful need for relationships, for support systems, systems that connect to a larger purpose. To that end, in organizations that focus solely on monetary rewards, while there may be an initial "spike" in motivation, very quickly people begin to distrust "authoritarian" leaders, eventually responding with apathy and deep disaffection.

There's just three things I ever say. If anything goes bad, then I did it. If anything goes semi-good, then we did it. If anything goes really good, then you did it. That's all it takes. (Coach Paul "Bear" Bryant)

In his classic *Leviathon,* Thomas Hobbes describes what he calls "the state of nature" as an anarchic situation in which all are compelled, for their survival, to engage in a ceaseless, continual struggle for power. About this "war of all against all," two important points should be made: that this Hobbesian view of the dangers of anarchy captured what he believed to be an important dimension of the human condition and that to call that condition "the state of nature" is just no longer valid. It may have been appropriate language centuries ago, but, because of free human choice, in today's civilized world, it is no longer a valid theory. I might add, parenthetically, that in many societies, many countries, even as we have entered the 21st century, many people still are robbed of the freedom to choose.

I'm reminded of the *three constants in life; change, free choice, and consequences of those choices.* And many people, in some countries, and in some organizations in America, involuntarily, or voluntarily, remain under the power and control of others. This language might make them feel a bit uncomfortable, but I believe it to be true. We have traded the uniqueness of humans for *control and power over people*; placing them in groups, so we don't have to deal with humans on a personal basis—essentially bartering our humanness for an exhausting love of efficiency. Now, I am not opposed to efficiency, when we are dealing with *things*; that is, doing things right, but effectiveness appeals to me more; because it deals with *human beings,* their creativity and imagination, the *fire within,* and doing the right things.

Efficiency is a *management* issue. You are dealing with *things*. Someone has to worry about and pay utility bills in an organization. Is that important? Yes, it is, quite important. Going into the office on Monday morning and switching on the electricity is important. What if it doesn't go on? You anticipate an unusually busy day, working several priorities, but your computer doesn't work. Is that a paradigm shift for you? You eventually discover that someone failed to pay the monthly utility bills.

That would clearly be a breakdown in management, not leadership. *Leadership* relates to human beings. Is *management* important? Yes, it is. But, we must follow *management* decisions with *leadership* decisions, for virtually everything relies on relationships.

In civilized societies, having escaped the control of nature, we must create controls, replacing the wholeness of nature through systems of ecological thinking, substituting for the law of nature, a human law. I submit that, until fairly recently in our country's history, certainly in the workplace, most people did not even believe that a world of love, honor, trust, and caring could exist. When Levi Strauss' CEO Robert Haas describes today's workplace, he says that "we are at the center of a seamless web of mutual responsibility/accountability/collaboration, a seamless partnership, with interrelationships and mutual commitments." Thus, the challenge for all of us is to use ethical, principle-based/centered power to significantly reduce or delimit coercive and/or utility power in relationships. Only then, can we be truly free.

> *A shift has occurred in organizational culture and the workplace over the last two decades. We all must try new things and learn to think in new ways. To innovate, we must learn not only to use new technologies, but to behave differently.* (Rosabeth Moss Kanter, January, 2002)

It's my view that, while we like to talk about trust, we have very little trust experience at a deep level. But most believe this behavioral trait is quite important. According to Gordon Shea, trust is not an abstract, theoretical, idealistic goal, forever beyond our reach. For it can be described as the "miracle ingredient in life, a lubricant that reduces friction, a bonding agent that glues together disparate parts, a catalyst that facilitates action. No substitute—neither threat nor promise, will do the job as well." Unconditional trust, an expression of faith, enhances security, reduces inhibitions and defensiveness, and allows people to share feelings and dreams. It permits you to put your deepest fears in the palms of the hands of others, knowing that they will be treated with care, because the relationship itself is highly valued.

Empowerment is one of the most popular *management/leadership* buzzwords and yet the least understood, most anxiety-provoking term in business today. And when most people speak of empowerment, they are thinking about relatively small shifts of power within a conventional hierarchical structure. Multi-dimensional in practice, psychological empowerment captures individual behavior; social empowerment, peer behavior, results in organizational empowerment. Jan Carlson, the CEO of Scandinavian Airlines, describes empowerment—insightfully—as "freeing someone from rigorous control by instruction, policies, and orders by creating an environment where that person becomes free to take responsibility for their ideas, decisions and actions. The result is a release of hidden resources that would otherwise remain inaccessible to both the individual and the organization." Thus, the key is that one cannot give empowerment to people. They have to choose to take it, but *empowerment is not abandonment*. One might require an investment in *additional training* (which is to push or force into individuals new skills/tools/competencies in order for them to be able to function efficiently/effectively, fulfilling necessary and appropriate duties) or *additional education* (pulling or forcing out of us ... qualities of leadership that we all have, but which are often just lying dormant). As an aside, I think we invest too much time and money in training, and too little time and money in education; just as I believe we traditionally focus too much on "teaching" and too little on "learning."

We have known for six decades that whenever formal annual performance appraisals are introduced into an organization, performance and productivity go down, yes, go down. They contribute to the *trivialization of the meaning of one's passion and contribution*. And yet many organizations still cling to these obsolete "instruments." They have essentially developed a functional blindness to their own dysfunction. I would go even further and say whenever a standard "bell" curve is used in organizations, where we choose to discriminate and compare humans and their performance, we make everyone "mentally ill." With the exception of very important and necessary "feedback," (measurement devices, which normally define what is meaningful), formal annual ratings never enhance human performance. Human beings choose to "self motivate" when they feel genuinely valued, discover their meaning in life, willingly struggle and create together in a common goal that they love. And then they truly connect with their chosen career, or profession, and to each other. Separating, and in a formal way, comparing and contrasting people, becomes a cultural pathology, breeding resentment, toxicity, and contempt in the organization; and, in my view, when we rely on these "tired" methods, we reinforce mediocrity.

If one would just think for a second, individuals are hired because they are seen as talented contributors, and then we start "weeding them out," comparing and contrasting them. What does this do to the culture? Now I am not suggesting that underachievers—*minimalists*—should be rewarded, quite the opposite. Individuals who choose not to grow, choose to invest about a third of their potential in advancing the organization; who choose not to create, not to learn, not to accept responsibility, and personal accountability must be invited to take their skills elsewhere. Keeping them sends a signal to the high achievers that it's okay to be a "minimalist." We must turn "brain numbing" bureaucracies into associations of citizens mutually committed to advancing the larger community, the larger good.

Mentally ill organizations, both public and private, that reward mediocrity and inhibit or prohibit normal human behavior reflect dysfunctionality and are hemorrhaging. And many of these organizations remain in denial. They just refuse to admit their continued manipulation and exploitation of humans. And, if they have not already, they will lose their competitiveness and become bankrupt. We know that intellectual capital, *brain power, creative juices* is where we need to invest our resources, not more brick and mortar. Organizational leaders (big "L" leaders) who are committed to excellence must create and nurture a culture that inspires and gives people the freedom to create, to imagine, to care, to build, and to take responsibility for their future. (And, yes, give people the freedom to fail, but they must, absolutely must, learn from their mistakes and choose not to repeat them, especially being reckless with resources.) Frankly, I rather enjoy being around people with *scars on their bodies* (not literally, necessarily). It demonstrates they have *screwed things up a bit on occasion.* For it is through mistakes that we learn. Being risk averse is not only irresponsible in organizations today; it is truly reckless and negatively impacts one's commitment to further emotional and intellectual growth.

To fully exploit the possibilities of new information technologies, global commerce, and the accelerating speed of changes in the workplace, we need to expand the concept of empowerment to include radically decentralized organizations, like the Internet, free markets of all kinds—all models for new ways of organizing community, stakeholder, and citizen activities in the twenty-first century. Thomas W. Malone describes *connected/decentralized/accountable* decision makers as the operative, optimum, model for the challenges of today. Sharing information with each other, these decentralized decision makers can combine the best information available anywhere in the world with their own knowledge, energy, and creativity.

According to Malone, "as the world's economy becomes increasingly dependent on creative innovation and knowledge work, and as new technologies make possible the connection of decentralized decision makers on a scale never before possible, exploiting such opportunities for local empowerment may well become one of the most important themes in economic history of this new century." Of course, this dynamic will be impacted by many imponderables, such as potential wars, government regulation, political turbulence, national and religious cultures, and natural calamities. What I think we can expect, and expect very quickly, is increasing frequency of and reliance upon *Virtual Teams, Virtual Offices, and Boundaryless Organizational Structures.* Having less office space, raising the ratio of employees to workstations, will, while giving stakeholders greater freedom to grow and contribute, clearly save considerable operational costs. This will occur at the same time that there is greater commitment and investment in *transformational out-sourcing*, the turning over of service activities, as a whole, or in part, to a third-party contractor; either on a transitional or a long-term basis. These services would range from legal to accounting, business processes, human resources management/development, staff training/education, food service, security, facilities maintenance/management, to information technology. The results will be greater organizational flexibility, reduction of costs, improving service, with a greater likelihood of "ownership," accountability, and empowerment with all stakeholders. This will allow the organization to concentrate on what they do well, their core competencies, and to leave the rest to someone else, to contractors who must consistently deliver truly quality service, or they will be replaced, and should be quite quickly.

> *About 40% of the company is now administration, finance, and backroom functions. Over the next three years, I want to shrink that by 75%.* (Jeff Immelt CEO, General Electric Corporation— January, 2002)

It constantly annoys me to hear about administrators "administrating" in organizations today. We don't need any more administrators. In fact, we could probably examine the depth and quality of "value added" contributions of the vast majority of these people, and conclude they do more harm than good. We need *liberators*, who will free the stakeholders—the citizens—in the organization to pursue greatness in their lives, and, concomitantly, advance their collective interests. According to Tom Peters, one of the more passionate, highly regarded, leadership "gurus," "we have to reinvent virtually every organization within the next five years." "Ninety percent of everything white collar workers do will be replaced by professional out-source centers." Well, I don't know about 90% being an accurate forecast, but certainly many divisions, departments, and profit and loss centers will be replaced by various professional service support specialists. In fact, with respect to personnel resource support, I believe the operative paradigm for the future will be not unlike professional athletes, where there are signing bonuses and specific contractual deliverables. These people will be affiliated with multiple organizations, simultaneously providing quality services, being compensated fairly with multiple revenue "steams," and being highly mobile, highly motivated, highly effective, and highly accountable.

Samuel Johnson, some 200 years ago, said "language is the dress of thought." And, Professor Charles Handy said "the way we talk colors the way we think, and the way we think shapes the way we act. In fact, we are the unconscious prisoners of our language." Dr. Handy believes corporations, as well as public organizations, should be regarded as communities, with a purpose beyond them to give them cohesion and motion. Corporations are not a piece of property. "Communities are created for a common purpose rather than a common place, something to which one belongs; while they, in turn, belong to no one." And the core members of every community should be more properly regarded as citizens rather than as employees or "human resources," as citizens with responsibilities as well as rights. In fact, while I have taught Human Resources Management classes for many years, because I choose to reject the notion that human beings are essentially commodities; "things" to be manipulated/used/exploited, I have always found the term(s) insulting and demeaning. We are not machines; inanimate objects. We are flesh and blood, miracles put on this earth by our creator; sharing the same fate—to serve each other, to make choices on how we create our destinies.

I share the same view as Dr. Handy that the generally accepted idea of a corporation being owned by its shareholders will eventually become obsolete. While investors in private corporations are certaintly entitled to due rewards for investing in the firms, this arrangement does not make clear where the real power lies. The real influence and power come from the people who have built and who are investing their ingenuity, innovativeness, and creativity to make the organization better and more profitable. The inspired workforce within organizations should not be treated as mere instruments of others. They desire to be enfranchised, for they really are the "owners" of the collective journey of advancing the organization's continued growth, while they themselves are also growing, emotionally, spiritually, and, hopefully, financially. The continuing challenge is that "all growth occurs while it's being inhibited" (Peter Senge). That's the overriding predicament that we find outselves in.

Be brave, relentless, fearless. Be courageous. Choose to be great; choose to give power away. Choose consistently to be honorable and hold in high esteem those who are honest, who manifest integrity in their beliefs and actions. Choose to be a person of integrity, patient in relationships; be gentle, kind. Be inclined not to manipulate others, accepting unconditionally your colleagues. True power comes from withholding judgment, requiring no evidence or specific performance as a condition for your treatment of others. Now I am not suggesting, in any way, that there not be consequences to all of life's choices, but we choose to do so out of genuine acceptance, warmth, concern, and caring.

The term "stakeholder," a democratic concept growing out of a pragmatic regard for the strength and celebration of diversity, has gained currency in the past decade or so as organization leaders have more acutely recognized the complex web of relationships that makes possible their success.

As previously mentioned, I served twenty-six years in an Air Force uniform, six of those years in the active Reserves (1974-1980); and the other twenty on active duty. During those six years, I was employed as a Senior Marketing Specialist with the Aerospace Group, Space Systems Division of General Electric (GE). It was while at GE that I recall and want to share my second "signature story"; one on empowerment which relates to a graduation address from Jack Welch. I believe it was in March of 1980 that I was privileged to have been selected to attend a three-week Marketing Workshop at Crotonville, New York, at GE's International Educational Institute. It was absolutely a terrific program. We were challenged every day to be at our very best and, after dinner, the teams would meet again for two or three hours to work on daily assignments. The faculty consisted of the "best and brightest" group of management and marketing professors from Harvard, Brown, and Columbia Universities. They truly were an impressive group of people.

Our graduation speaker at the end of the three weeks was Mr. Jack Welch, a gentleman whom we had heard was the personal selectee of Reg Jones, the current CEO, who would be retiring shortly. Now, Reg Jones was a real treasure within the corporation. He was leaving a powerful legacy of visionary leadership and leaving a corporation that was highly profitable and highly diversified, with global reach. However, Reg knew there were future challenges, storm clouds on the horizon because of increasing global competition and new technologies being introduced into the workforce, which would potentially displace many GE employees.

Preceding Jack Welch's arrival at Crotonville was his reputation, a reputation of excellence, in every position he served in within the corporation. We had heard he was quite demanding of everyone in his organizations and would not tolerate mediocrity. We also discussed his competitive spirit. An example was his addiction to and affection for one of the most personally humbling of all individual sports, the game of golf, where he shot regularly "par golf," which is a remarkable feat of skill.

We were waiting for his arrival that Friday morning outside the auditorium where the graduation ceremony was to be held. And, right on schedule, Jack drove up in a really "sporty" Alpha Romeo Spyder Veloce roadster. Looking pretty "dapper," Jack jumped out, introduced himself and instantly won us over as a guy you would want to hang around with. This fellow, not physically imposing, but unmistakably really focused, was exuding confidence, a person really comfortable "within his skin." He just smiled, shook a few hands and said, "Let's get started." After convening, he stood up in front of the group, gave us a quick summary of the Corporation's strategic posture, and said, "I'll now take your questions." We were quite taken by his apparent speech impediment. Jack had a pronounced stutter, which he has since overcome, to the point that it is not noticeable.

During the Q & A period, very predictably, Jack was painfully honest and candid. With this guy what you saw, was what you got; absolutely authentic, bone honesty. All eyes were focused on this one guy. Jack expected excellence from all of us and would not tolerate anything less than our total commitment to advancing the corporation. This guy was absolutely "radioactive" with energy. But now this was some twenty-two years ago; he said the following, "I want the employees of General Electric Corporation to be rewarded both in the pocketbook and the soul. GE will be the best worldwide in all of our businesses." While this was, needless to say, most intriguing to the attendees, some nine years later, when he spoke of a "boundaryless" organization, this was truly a paradigm shift in thinking.

General Electric will become a boundaryless company, with no inside barriers, knocking down external walls, making suppliers and customers part of a single process. It will eliminate the less visible walls of race and gender, putting the team ahead of individual ego. (Jack Welch, December, 1989)

We all agreed those were laudable goals, but certainly WOW statements. In fact, we had never heard anything quite so compelling for a future CEO to share with employees. Of course, today, many organizations, certainly the more successful, reflect these paradigms. Then, Jack was on a roll. Becoming animated, with his voice rising, Jack said the culture within GE would ultimately change, because the times were changing. He said, which everyone knew anyway, that the old days of life-time employment was over. He couldn't guarantee anyone ten years, or ten months with GE. But there was one thing he could guarantee, and that was, when you left GE, you were going to be a more important, more significant, more valuable asset to your next employer. And, if you think about it, that's really not a bad deal.

Jack said there must be an acceptance of greater demands being placed on all. We are going to be asked to do a lot of things, and we must do them well. The days of the "technocrat"—an expert in just one narrow area where you were three feet wide and a mile deep is over. You had to be a mile wide and about three foot deep. You had to choose to do a lot of things reasonably well, and you had to understand the power and strength of TEAM. We understood what he meant. Essentially, he gave us a professorial sermon on what would happen within the company. He said rather than an issue of change, there would be significant transitions within the corporation. Jack made the distinction between changes being situational, external (a new boss or new plant location) and transitions being psychological, internal (which would be more challenging). And he believed unless the transition were successful, any change would not be permanent, but at best, temporary, which to him, would not be tolerated.

I was familiar with this concept, remembering it from graduate school, where a *transition starts with an ending, and a beginning with letting go of something.* The difficult part is letting go. The second step is understanding what comes after the letting go, the neutral zone between old reality and the new. The old way is gone, and the new doesn't quite feel comfortable yet. If you escape prematurely from the neutral zone, you compromise the opportunity to alter or modify behavior, with no chance for any successful transition to occur. To encourage all of your stakeholders (employees) to choose to embrace new ways of thinking and higher expectations on their performance, you must create the conditions where this has a high chance of success. And it must be done when people in the organization are uncertain about their future and when they realize that the "lifelong employment" covenant which had been somewhat traditional within GE was soon to end. Most living things, certainly, humans will transition, will change if the alternative is worse than the change, or they see change as the means of preserving themselves. *It's really the challenge of not getting new thoughts into people's brains, but getting old ideas out. Forgetting* would be the issue! Now, how do you do this?

You first identify who is losing what, not being surprised when people will "overreact," some reaching literally a panic state. You must acknowledge the losses openly, sympathetically, and compassionately,then finally expect and accept signs of grieving, not unlike what one would observe at a funeral. This latter stage will require most of the stakeholders to go through several transitions—anger, bargaining, anxiety, sadness, disorientation, then finally for many, a state of depression. Thus, very predictably, thousands of displaced people went through the stages of guilt, resentment, anxiety, self-absorption, and, finally, stress. Now, I will add here, that GE was apparently quite financially generous in its separation policies and was very aggressive in continuing to finance higher education, new training, as well as helping people find new employment. Even though, during the first five years of Jack Welch's tenure at GE, some one fourth of the employee force was displaced, their competitors in their respective industries knew these people were very talented and extremely "employable." Thus, while some entered retirement, many, if not most, found other employment fairly quickly, with GE selling businesses to other corporations, or they were recruited by competitors.

Jack has written and spoken many times about how difficult many of these decisions were closing plants, selling off entire divisions within the company, knowing how potentially disruptive this would be to so many families. But he felt it must done, and done fairly quickly, if GE were to continue to be the global leader in so many different industries. Again, Jack and his select team of high-powered servant leaders repeatedly clarified and communicated the PURPOSE for this transition, painting a PICTURE of how the outcome would look and feel, laying out a PLAN for phasing in the outcome, and, best as they could, explaining the importance of this turbulent period: essentially, the world had changed, and GE had to change with it. Our *past successes* will *not guarantee future success.*

> *A manager has come to mean someone who controls rather than facilitates, complicates rather than simplifies, acts more like a governor than an accelerator. ... What we are trying to develop is an effervescent culture that crackles with creativity. We are trying to become a $60 billion global company with the fire and zest, the heart and soul, of a start-up.* (Jack Welch, January, 1985)

Jack's message was clear, passionate, and unambiguous. High performers, people who deliver on commitments and are trustworthy, will be rewarded, will be given the freedom to pursue excellence, but the low performers may be asked to leave. And then he went on to say the following, "And I don't care how good you are technically; if you cannot get along with other members of your team, if you do not respect diversity, if you are not a person of integrity, if you are a negative influence in the organization, if you are not trustworthy, if you do not show respect and treat your teammates with dignity, irrespective of your technical strengths, it's problematic that your tenure will continue with the company. Your retention is not worth the price." He said, "we no longer have the luxury of carrying water for you. Either you choose to modify your behavior, or you must leave. We wish you well." Again, we all agreed these were pretty WOW observations. At that point, "we were ready to take the hill." Jack spoke for about an hour, then we adjourned for a bit of fellowship and a luncheon. Afterwards, he made it a point to shake all of our hands, asked us to stay in touch with his office, let him know our thoughts on how things were going, and wished us continued success at GE. What I was left with was the obvious. This guy was radioactive and what you saw was what you got, warts and all. Since that March, 1981 date, and the event up in Crotonville, Jack Welch did what he set out to do; change the culture of General Electric, and although he retired about a year ago, he still remains one of the legendary corporate leaders of the past two decades.

> *Nothing is unchangeable but the inherent and inalienable rights of man.* (Thomas Jefferson)

In order to pursue and acquire true personal and professional alignment, and a sense of self-fulfillment in committing ourselves to our chosen profession, we must be a stakeholder and active participant, an owner who desires accountability for the choices we make. In fact, you shouldn't choose to be around people who don't have an appetite for personal and professional accountability. It tends to be fatiguing and eventually corrodes the relationship. It could literally become toxic. You can choose your attitude about those things over which you have no control. The statement of Allan Massie reinforces this important principle of what I am speaking: *"We are responsible for actions performed in response to circumstances for which we are not responsible."* To acquire excellence today in our lives, we must hold ourselves accountable. Choose not to be a victim, embracing a "victimology" that has become almost epidemic in many organizations today. And I would suggest that these organizations that allow for, that excuse or condone this "toxicity," will become former organizations very quickly.

You don't hire people who "just sell fried chicken." This is cruel, humiliating; it denies one their dignity and sense of self-worth. And it is also demonstrably ineffective. You must attract and retain the great contributors, and create and nurture an organizational culture where individuals are truly inspired to acquire ownership, trust unconditionally people with superior interpersonal skills who have an appetite for pursuing excellence, and have a passion to embrace empowerment and achieve both personal and professional alignment in their lives. I am not suggesting that some training is not appropriate on occasion. These are technical competencies that, indeed, might be necessary to provide the skilled, enlightened workforce you need, especially in the information systems arena. But I suggest it's education that is the "force multiplier." It's intellectual capital which will be the dominant competitive weapon of this century, as well as a deep understanding that we must make mutual investments and support in all relationships, essentially a commitment away from dependency and independency and toward the more mature posture of interdependence. *The belief in one's separate existence is an optical delusion* (Albert Einstein).

You should avoid choosing to be an obstructionist, rude, difficult to get along with, one who prides themselves on fierce independence. Now, I am not talking about committed workers who questions policies; who question procedures; who suggest different approaches, different paradigms, different models to rely on as the organization pursues excellence. These people need to be protected and encouraged to express themselves, not to be reckless with resources, but to take risks; to explore different ways to attack issues, different ways of seeking and creating solutions. And although they will, on occasion, try things that don't work, mistakes are the windows of discovery. Bertrand Russell reminded, us, *"Do not fear to be eccentric in opinion, for every opinion now accepted was once eccentric."*

Today in organizations committed to excellence, we do not have the luxury of keeping people on the payroll who are just darn difficult to work with, creating negative synergy, irrespective of their technical strengths. And just having a good work ethic is not good enough today. We have to think differently and understand that the "team is the hero" today. All of us are more important than any of us. Inviting people who are totally out of alignment with values and principles, and who do not understand we must sublimate and subordinate our own personal agendas to advance the larger good, the larger community, truly should take their skills elsewhere. Workers today must understand that whatever made them successful may not, or will no longer, work. When an individual or any organization decides that success has been attained, most, if not all, progress stops. Dr. Peter Vail recently stated that "you cannot coast on the knowledge base you have acquired thus far in your life." I could not agree more with that view. *Because of brutal competition in the workplace today, we no longer can tolerate people, albeit with wonderful brains, brains that start working the moment they get up in the morning, then choose to shut their brains off when they get to work.* They are going to be or are a drain on the organization. Advising them to take their skills elsewhere is a very caring thing to do. Wish them well. Maybe they can find other employment where their dysfunctional and rather mis-aligned behavior is more readily accepted.

Thus, you should not obsess with the *bottom line*. Focus on the *top line*, investing in your team, your stakeholders. The profits will come. Trust that they will do a good job, and, with very few exceptions, they will do a good job. Those "exceptional" instances where they choose not to might require some intervention; intervention that will result in their seeking employment elsewhere. It just takes honesty, courage, and continued commitment to excellence on your part. And, with respect to giving your team power, you know you don't want someone on you all the time. Be certain that they take ownership of the "vision", the stated strategic goals of your organization. Be patient, trust them, and give them freedom to breathe, so they can be creative, innovative, and imaginative. They won't let you down. And the *bottom line* will take care of itself. The following fact, with a truly powerful message, about natural law and how we choose to learn from ecology, is shared: *The Chinese bamboo tree, when planted, grows for some four years, beneath the surface, grows down and out. It never breaks the surface of the ground. During the fifth year, it grows to a height of eighty feet.*

Thus, like the Chinese bamboo tree, invest in relationships. Plant the seed; be patient; trust and have faith in the potential of those around you. Raise that high bar on your desire to pursue and acquire greatness … and expect it from those around you. Is it easy? No, it is quite difficult, and will require great courage and commitment to excellence on your part.

In Dr. Blaine Lee's *The Power Principle*, he describes and examines the four power models/paradigms in relationships or in organizations today. The first, *powerlessness*, captures those individuals who truly feel they have absolutely no self esteem, worth, or value. The least mature model, this behavior reflects a rather masochistic view of life. They are dependent on others, or someone, or some thing for their welfare, their livelihood, their personal growth, sometimes, even their survival. They live a life of fear. The second model, *coerciveness* occurs when one individual feels someone or something (possibly an organization) "owns" them, not unlike property. They are being coerced to do what they feel is demanded of them. If you choose to violate this perceived contract or covenant, you will be arbitrarily separated from this relationship. This power model is fatiguing, toxic, corrosive, and, ultimately, destructive. Like the first model, you also fear being detached, dismissed, divorced from the relationship. The third power model, *utility or utilitarian*, is one where you feel accepted/desired in the relationship, as long as you "produce." It's "what have you done for me lately? Or I will keep you around just as long as you pleasure or please me." Because, at that point where you are, indeed, not pleasing a very important or key person, you are discarded, replaced, essentially traded in for someone else. The fourth model, reflecting the most mature qualities and requiring the greatest strength of character, is *principle-centered or principle-based.* It captures powerfully the foundational principles of honor, integrity, dignity, fidelity, truly, the uniqueness of the human experience. The first, and most important, of the principles is always honor; for if you "fail to honor people, they will fail to honor you." (Lao-Tzu, Sixth Century, B.C.E.) The relationship investments should be mutual. Both of us are stronger than any one of us, and we therefore live a much more rich and fulfilling life. The fourth model relies on the tenets attributed, respectively, to Mohandas Gandhi and Eleanor Roosevelt, "No one can take away your self-respect if you do not give it to them," and "Nothing can make you feel inferior without your consent."

In a recently published journal article, Oren Harari has formulated a point-by-point guide to *Colin Powell's Seven Laws of Power.* Secretary Powell would certainly not remember an incident, back in the mid-'80's, when I heard a knock on the door of one of the private dining rooms at the Pentagon. I walked over and opened the door. And WOW, I saw General Colin Powell. He smiled and asked if this was the luncheon he was scheduled to attend. I said, "General, unfortunately, no. We would love to host you, but I think your luncheon is next door." He asked, "What's going on in here?" I told him about our luncheon and who the attendees were. He said; "Gee, I'd love to join you, but, you're probably right. I'd better get to my luncheon. You guys, enjoy." I thought what presence, what posture. I immediately felt this man was anchored, was truly centered. And when polls are taken today which ask what Americans we most admire, Secretary Powell seems to be always on top. Here are *Colin Powell's Seven Laws of Power* that Oren Harari describes:

1. Dare To Be the Skunk. "Every organization should tolerate rebels who tell the emperor he has no clothes."

2. To Get the Real Dirt, Head For the Trenches. "The people in the field are closest to the problem." Trust the opinions of people you serve.

3. Share the Power. "Plans don't accomplish work. It's people who get things done." Every job is important and all people have vital roles to perform.

4. Know When To Ignore Your Advisers. "Experts often possess more data than judgment."

5. Develop Selective Amnesia. "Too many leaders get so trapped in fixed ways of seeing things that they can't cope when the situation changes."

6. Come Up For Air . "I don't have to prove to anybody that I can work sixteen hours a day if I can get it done in eight."

7. Declare Victory and Quit. "Command is lonely, and so is the decision to withdraw from the position of authority. Leadership is not rank, privilege, titles, or money. It's responsibility."

It is suggested that the fuel that drives so many aspects of human conduct ... is the insatiable desire for power. The desire for power is inherent in our very nature and fundamental to our survival as a species on this earth. And nowhere is the pursuit of power more evident than in today's workplace. Many people have an obvious appetite to constantly strive to increase their arsenal for power. And while some may use power for selfish gain, others may legitimately use it to benefit their organizations. Unfortunately, many leaders assume that there is a limited, finite supply of power, that giving power to another means diminishing one's own power. But, I believe the capricious use of power breaks down and perturbates the normal channels of communication between the visionary, visible, senior leaders and others in the organization. And this ultimately means the deterioration and lessening of power and influence.

It seems to me that most people contribute only a small fraction of their full capabilities, simply because they do not feel a sense of personal power. I have given hundreds of workshops and seminars on "Leadership and Power," working with literally thousands of individuals, and it's very rare when any participant tells me that they use all of their talents in the workplace.

Find a purpose in life so big it will challenge your every capacity to be at your best. (David O. McKay)

In organizations truly committed to excellence, the "scorched earth" policy of management and leadership, which reflects sheer cowardship and lack of honesty and courage, is not tolerated. It lies in the dust pan of history. It's over. Let it go. Organizations that are swimming in a culture of mediocrity soon will be hemorrhaging, and will die a slow death. They remain in a state of denial. The new paradigm of effective leadership is one of caring, trusting unconditionally, investing in your workforce (both in training and education), being humble, and not just valuing differences, but celebrating differences, and not just different cultures, races, people of different religions, but respecting and seeking out different ideas. And, at the same time, holding yourself and those around you to a very high standard of conduct, of behavior—personal and professional—to one of accountability. Commit yourself to honesty of words and deeds. As cited in Stephen Covey's insightful and very popular *Seven Habits of Highly Effective People,* choose to be principle-centered; adhering to tenets of fairness, justice, fidelity, trust, and integrity. There are self-evident, self-validating natural laws that operate regardless of whether we decide to obey them or not. They are always there, always reliable, and provide direction in our lives and in our organizations. They provide strength and real power, the power to create our destiny. With respect to the use of power, the following insightful quotation is not speaking of gender. Ms. Thatcher is speaking about what real power is—or is not.

If you have to tell someone you're a lady ... you're not.

There is empirical evidence that if you choose to commit yourself and reflect the highest standards of honesty and personal propriety, people will choose to listen to you, and you don't know they are listening to you. People will be watching you, and you don't know they're watching you. Create this "zone of peace" around you. And, not unlike a magnet, it will draw people to your zone of influence. *And the secret to influencing positively a large group is you. It begins with one person.*

I think Peter Senge had it right, when he recently said, "The operative paradigm of effective leadership today is that it must capture the capacity of a human community to sustain significant change." Thus, it does not reside in individual workers. It resides in the community. Empowerment in all aspects of our lives occurs when we commit to improving everyday in every aspect of our lives, and when we encourage and expect those around us to share this view. Is this easy? No, it's very difficult. It requires courage, commitment, and belief in the power of interdependence. *You can command as long as you can enforce. You can lead through logic as long as you can persuade and convince. But you can always lead if people believe.*

When asked why he worked so hard, and seemingly so passionate, author and prominent motivational speaker on "Love and Profit," James Autry, said, "I love to turn the key in the door and put on the coffee pot." Love of their products, love of their teammates in the workplace, love of their customers, (and relating this theme to Shenandoah University), love of their students, love of their profession—this may just be the best-kept secret of exemplary servant leadership.

Once more into the breach, dear friends, once more—follow your spirit, and upon this charge, cry God for Harry, England, and Saint George. (William Shakespeare, *The Life of King Henry V*)

So, what is it that makes us go riding into the breach, following those leaders who don't have William Shakespeare writing their speeches? Some would argue that the answer is charisma, *gravitas*, and either you have it or you don't. I don't think it's that simple. I was so fortunate in military and corporate careers to have personally observed many leaders who could not be described as charismatic by any sort of rhetorical stretch, but they nevertheless managed to inspire an enviable trust and intense loyalty in their fellow teammates. And through their personal, their principle-based power; their ability to inspire people around them to pursue and achieve greatness, they were able to effect necessary changes in the culture of their organizations and make real their guiding visions. Their own belief in and enthusiasm for the vision are the spark that ignites the flame of inspiration. These people are always campaigning, articulating a vision that inspires pursuit of excellence. They are early adopters of innovation, of truly *trusting with no conditions*, aware that we often let each other down. They are clearly brave enough to fail as leaders. Every step they regard as a learning opportunity; they learn from their mistakes, as well as their successes. Leo Buscaglia put it this way:

> *I'm often met with cynicism because of my positive and passionate approach to trusting. I learned long ago to ignore the accusation that I am foolish and naive because of this. It continues to astound me how agitated some people get when I explain my belief that trust unites and secures as nothing else can; that without it, love cannot possibly endure. It doesn't seem to me that this is such an outrageous proposition, really, but it does seem to bring forth the detractors.*

> *When we cease trusting, negative forces take over. Good intentions go unappreciated in minds crowded with doubt and suspicion. Expressions of love are suspected of having hidden meanings. Everyday behavior gives rise to monumental traumas. We worry that we will be deceived if we trust too much, yet do not consider the consequences of not trusting enough.*

Dr. Warren Bennis, Professor of Management at the University of Southern California, believes the underlying issue in leadership is trust, a trait of human behavior that cannot be taught. It can only be learned. In fact, trust is the underlying issue not only in getting people on your side, but more importantly, in having them stay there. And how do we do that?

- Exercise constancy. Stay the course.

- Exercise congruity. Servant Leaders must walk their talk. There is no gap between the theories they espouse and the life they practice.

- Exercise reliability. Servant Leaders are there when it counts, supporting their teammates and associates in the moments that matter

- Exercise integrity. Servant Leaders honor their commitments and promises.

Thus, embracing constancy, congruity, reliability, and integrity secures a wholeness that encompasses the belief system on such a deep level that it is impossible to divorce what we believe from how we act. These qualities reflect a believing, thinking, speaking, and behaving in complete adherance to personal and professional values and principles. Many times when people act in a way that is not congruent with their deep beliefs, values, and principles, they do so not with intent but because they lack clarity about what they believe at heart or because conflicting beliefs create confusion within themselves and send mixed messages to others. This "misalignment" potentially results in a great deal of personal stress within themselves and less than clear communication with others, which could result in a perceived lack of integrity. The key is wisdom almost as old as dirt. It is to know thyself. Lao-Tzu, in the sixth century, stated, *"He who conquers others is strong; he who conquers himself is mighty."*

So, how do you rate when using power? On a scale of 1-10, would you give yourself a high mark, maybe an 8 or a 9? You understand that power is given to you, and it will be appropriately taken from you if you abuse it. Do you believe that truly *powerful* people give the greatest respect to their colleagues? They honor all and treat others with great dignity. Or, would you score yourself on the low end of the spectrum, maybe a 2 or a 3? You believe that you have to control others. You have difficulty trusting people.

Choose to avoid this controlling appetite and choose to trust people, unconditionally. Choose to pursue greatness today.

Let me now invite you to explore *principle #5, prioritizing your life*. As you review the material, be mindful of how you might score yourself, on a scale of 1-10. If you are on the low end, you are just beaten down by life's challenges, pressures, stresses. You feel oxygen starved at times, similar to the feeling you get when you are at the beach, and the rolling surf just keeps knocking you down. But, if you score high on the scale, around 8 or above, you have found true alignment, and are able to deal with the turbulence, confusion, instability, and uncertainty that surrounds you. It's your choice.

It is never too late to be what you might have been.

— George Eliot

5

PRIORITIZE YOUR LIFE

No horse gets anywhere until he is harnessed. No steam or gas ever drives anything until it is confined. No Niagara is ever turned into light and power until it is tunneled. No life ever grows until it is focused, dedicated, disciplined.

— Henry Emerson Fosdick

In the mid-eighties, I was Head Coach of a Little League Pee Wee Baseball team, for kids ages 6-8. I worked with my kids, including my young son, and forcefully instructed them, over and over: "If you hit the ball, don't run smugly to first base, stop and wave at your parents." "No, you hit the ball; you go to second." At every practice, I would drum it into their little heads. I strongly believed if you didn't stretch, you didn't grow. "You hit the ball. You go to second. If you get thrown out, that's okay. We'll get them next time."

It was my third year as Coach, when my son was eight years old, and a remarkable incident happened. After some three weeks of practice, it was time for the big game. It was a glorious Saturday morning at Catoctin Elementary School in Leesburg, Virginia. A huge crowd had gathered: moms, dads, siblings, grandmas, grandpas, uncles, aunts, neighbors, friends. Helicopters were coming in from all over the East Coast. ("Just kidding.") (Although it was clearly ... "tense city.") The stands were full. The big moment had arrived.

Now, as I mentioned, we had practiced for three weeks, roughly five times a week. My first batter that Saturday morning was a young 6-year-old, whose parents had recently moved to Leesburg. He was a good athlete; a bit nervous about being the first batter. And, undoubtedly, many of his family members were in the stands. As Head Coach, I had the responsibility of operating the pitching machine, and the task of putting the ball over the plate to my batters. Holding my breath, hoping I would be able to throw a strike directly over the plate, the machine responded marvelously. The nervous youngster swung hard, connecting sharply with the ball, resulting in a solid grounder between second and third base, followed by an enormous ovation from the stands.

But where did the youngster go? Undoubtedly excited, he immediately made a mad dash *directly* to second base, running right past me on the pitcher's mound, literally coming within inches of where I was standing. He was so intent on making it to second base safely, he didn't even notice my presence on the mound. It was clearly one of those wonderful moments that become "hard-wired" in our memory drum, a moment that makes life fulfilling.

Needless to say, the crowd went absolutely crazy, howling in disbelief. People were laughing, crying, choking, literally stunned. The umpire was not able to speak coherently. It was up to me, the Head Coach, to walk back to second base and tell the youngster he was out. Standing on second base, smiling broadly, waving at his parents, he quickly realized something wasn't quite right. The players on the other team started laughing at him, and he became confused. Advising him that he was out, he said: "But, Coach, I did what you told me to do." "Yeah, I know," I said, "But, you have to go to first base ... first."

Besides the noble art of getting things done, there is the noble art of leaving things undone. The wisdom of life lies in eliminating the nonessentials. (Chinese proverb)

So, what is your first base? It should be reflected in one's life mission statement; what gives your life its sense of relevance and purpose? Until you come to grips with what gives your life its meaning, achieving true fulfillment, both personally and professionally, is problematic. To that end, what are your priorities in life? What are those things that mean more than anything else in your life?

The great and glorious masterpiece of man is how to live with a purpose. (Michel de Montaigne)

One's life mission statement should be in two parts; the first, your *personal or family philosophy*; and the second, your *personal or family strategy*. The first speaks to a declaration of first, truly universal principles by which we can choose to live our lives; that is, honor, integrity, honesty, fidelity, faithfulness, fairness, belief in justice, and trustworthiness. This part captures the essence of your and/or your family's inner self. The second part, which should cover at least some ten years or so, speaks to how you will make your philosophy come alive, your strategic roadmap which lays out what needs to be done to insure your life's mission will be achieved. Is this important? Irvin D. Yalom offers the following, "Not to take possession of your life plan is to let your existence be an accident." Metaphorically, choose to program you life's computer.

The vital task rarely must be done today, or even this week. The urgent task calls for instant action. The momentary appeal of these tasks seems irresistible and they devour our energy. But in the light of time's perspective, their deceptive prominence fades. With a sense of loss we recall the vital task we pushed aside. We realize we've become slaves to the tyranny of the urgent. (Charles Hummel)

I have given Leadership Workshops all over the world, in many different cultures. And, without exception, when I ask my seminar participants to list those things that are most important to them, truly their priorities in life, they always list relationships, certainly beginning with the one we have with ourselves. But just discussing our priorities is not good enough. You must write these down. List them in your Weekly *"Prioritizer,"* your Organizer. They become, essentially a contract, and will take on greater importance when viewed and reviewed daily.

If you don't know where you're going, any road will take you there. (Author unknown)

Priority living is not a fad. It's not something that I believe will slowly pass into history. It's really something that we've known about for a long time, but we don't choose to do it. We prefer, still, a reliance upon managing or planning our schedules, an attempt to manage our time. It is suggested that you embrace a totally different approach, but it will require commitment and self discipline on your part. Essentially, *you schedule your priorities.* Now, I cannot tell you what your priorities are, other than, as I have previously discussed, say that they will relate to relationships and results. And, as Dr. Stephen Covey suggests, rather than focus on a clock, focus on a compass—because *where you are headed is more important than how fast you're going.* Thus, forget this silliness about managing time. If you think about it, that's impossible. One cannot manage time. We all get 24 hours a day, even though sometimes we deserve at least 30. But, guess what? There is a universal global standard of 24 hours. Thus, rather than managing time, let's choose to manage ourselves; or, better yet, lead ourselves, focusing on investing in relationships, the various roles that we have (son, daughter, parent, husband, wife, teacher, student, neighbor, parishoner, certainly starting with ourselves). *How many people on their deathbed wish they had spent more time at the office? Think. Think hard.*

It's my understanding that some 80-85% of money corporations invest, is spent on task-oriented issues, yet the research of human performance is quite clear. Some 80-85% of problems encountered in today's workplace involve people and relationships. This is evident even when the vast majority of jobs that exist today, involve the use of computer technology. Relationships are more important than things. These aren't just nice words. Evidence is overwhelming if we would just open our eyes and not continue to deny this fact.

So, how do we prioritize our lives, placing far more emphasis on the importance of relationships? Too many of us are scripted to believe we have to "find time" to do things. We don't "find time." Let's not be silly with *tired language.* No one can "find" time. We all get 24 hours, whether we need them or not. We don't manage time. We should choose to devote and dedicate ourselves to those things that are important to us, principally, relationships, starting with the one you have with yourself. And anything less than a conscious, deliberate commitment to the important is an unconscious, deliberate commitment to the unimportant.

Now, why don't traditional "time management" models work? There is no empirical evidence that traditional time management procedures, which suggest we work harder, smarter, and faster, will help us gain control over our life. It is suggested that, rather than focusing on time and things, we emphasize relationships and results. Antoine de Saint-Exuperty told us that "there is no hope of joy except in human relations." Instead of focusing solely on efficiency, doing things the right way, we must emphasize effectiveness, which means doing the right things and consistently pursuing and acquiring whatever assets we most desire. Dr. Peter Drucker reminds us that "there is nothing so useless as doing efficiently that which should not be done at all." We must connect the investment of time to our deeper priorities in life.

The tragedy of life doesn't lie in not reaching your goal. The tragedy lies in having no goal to reach. (Benjamin Mays)

There is a terrific story attributed to Horst Schultz, President and CEO of Ritz-Carlton Hotels. In 1996, they were honored as the beneficiary of the Deming Prize and recognized as *the Best Hotel in America.* Following the announcement, Ritz-Carlton Hotels celebrated this honor by holding a huge party at their corporate headquarters. As they were celebrating, their very popular President chose to speak to the throng of revelers. After wild applause, he spoke. Anticipating congratulatory praise, they were in for a surprise. President Schultz said, "Let's all enjoy the fellowship tonight." But then he hesitated and said with considerable conviction, "So, my friends, you think you're good? You're really lousey. On a scale of one to ten, you're about a four." And after a very long pause—which seemed like an hour to many of the guests—he said with a smile, "But you're a lot less lousy than you were last year. You must know we've got to do better—and we will." He was essentially saying, in order to get better in all of our various roles in life, we need to prioritize how we live our lives, and we need to serve—and to serve better—our guests at Ritz-Carlton Hotels.

With respect to "managing time," which really doesn't make much sense, we need to manage ourselves, taking responsibility for how we choose to allocate, devote, and prioritize our choices during the 24 hours in a day. The following are five historical stages of "time management" models that are offered for your consideration:

- The first model is one where you just live your life, day to day, based on how you feel; keeping in mind some sense of where your next meal is coming from, where you normally sleep at night, just responding to other people's expectations and assumptions on how you devote your life's attention; essentially a life of just bumping into things, a victim of other people's demands upon you. Unwittingly, you have just embraced a rather exhausting lifestyle of "victimization." This model, unfortunately, just might be the most common one today.

- The second model, an improvement over the first, is one where you have little "reminders," essentially "post-it" notes stuck on your refrigerator or steering wheel. These little checklists, if you choose to look at them, will provide some notion of what you have identified as important activities that deserve your attention. Of course, as we all have experienced, this is a problematic model at best, because just knowing what we have identified as things that are important rarely results in consistent behavioral change. There is no commitment to priority living with this model. I believe following this model reflects the insight of La Bruyese: "Those who make the worst use of their time are the first to complain of its brevity."

- The third model is based on "planning and preparation." This model is an improvement over the previous one, but still relies upon calendars and appointment books. Characteristics of this model include awkward-ness, inconsistency, and lack of alignment between what is truly important and what is deemed unimportant. Following this model leaves us jumping from one urgent issue to another, many of which are truly not important, are not in alignment with our values and principles.

- The fourth model is based on "planning, prioritizing, and controlling." This model is an improvement over the third, but still relies on the ineffectiveness of planners and traditional organizers, electronic as well as paper. It relies on a foundation of daily planning, which, today, as we know, is filled with unscheduled meetings, phone calls, annoying and inane distractions and memos. These leave us in a state of anxiety, never able to respond to covering or responding to the more important issues of the day, namely, relationships. This model is still too inflexible, too rigid, and even unnatural.

- The fifth, and I believe the optimum, operative model, captures the strengths of the other four, but eliminates their weaknesses. It really is a paradigm shift, a level of life leadership, a fundamental break with less effective ways of thinking and behaving. This model requires you to identify the most important things in your life, in all of your various roles. These are your priorities in life, all dealing with relationships. Once you have done that, write them down; then plan weekly, organizing and executing around these priorities. Although you plan weekly, you should view your daily activities in the context of lifetime dreams, goals, and roles.

We are a society of notoriously unhappy people—people who are glad when we have killed the time we are trying hard to save. (Erich Fromm)

Dr. Blaine Lee, in many of his *Power Principle* Workshops, asks his participants to identify what is necessary to grow terrific tomatoes. (Dr. Lee, I hope you don't mind my sharing your little exercise with my readers.) My University is located in the Shenandoah Valley of Northwest Virginia, truly a beautiful and glorious part of America. This area is known as *apple country*. Thus, I am choosing to replace the tomato with an apple. Truly, one of the many qualities and attributes that you find in this beloved part of Virginia is the large number of apple and vegetable farms. The exercise is called "How Do We Grow Delicious Apples in the Shenandoah Valley?" I think you will find it quite enlightening for it relates to the issue of how we choose to prioritize our lives.

The exercise is introduced and workshop participants are advised that we want to grow the largest, best apples in the world. We are preparing for the "Apple Growing Olympics," and we intend to win, having hired the best trained, credentialed, and experienced apple growers in the world. Participants are asked to just speak up as they choose, sharing with me and your colleagues what they need to do to grow huge, olympic-sized apples. As each item is mentioned, they are written on the board for all to see. Very predictably, the comments start flying. Predictably, participants shout out the need for the best seeds, seedlings, soil, stakes, fertilizer, pesticides, rainfall, weather, fencing, "tender loving care," pruning, weed clearing, and timing of the planting.

After a few minutes, when the participants have exhausted every possible idea that they have, ideas that will insure we indeed will have a hugely successful crop of "olympic-sized" apples, the following question is asked, "Now, if I do exactly what you advise, and do it quite well, is it guaranteed that we will have a marvelous crop of huge apples? They typically hesitate briefly, then say, "Well, of course not." I then say, "Why not? I have done everything you have asked of me; and, with the help of my crack team of expert apple growers, we have been passionate about following your instructions." "Now, again, why cannot I guarantee that we will have huge apples?" "Well, you just can't." Again, I say, " Why not?" Then, in the room, there is silence, and Blaine says, "Can I guarantee life to that seed?" "No." "Because the life of the seed is already there." And, in the language of this author, with respect to human behavior, I submit that ... that *"fire within"* ... is already there. It just rests on your choice to discover it.

That *"fire within"* all of us is reflected in passion and compassion—and how we choose to live our lives. What are our priorities, those things, those activities that are indeed important to us, important in strengthening a bond of trust and trustworthiness in relationships? For relationships are all there is. As former American Red Cross President Elizabeth Dole so aptly put it; "when the river is rising and it's 2:00 a.m., that's not the time to start a relationship."

The story about growing big apples is a neat little analog, a message about the potential power within all of us. And it is through our set of choices that we can "recover" and energize that power, for it is lying dormant in all of us. And, with too many people, that power is never revealed, never fully expressed. Our growth is too often stunted, emotionally and spiritually; thus, we are deprived of life's precious gift of the ability to love others as ourselves.

Loneliness and Love

> *To fully relate to another, one must first relate to oneself. If we cannot embrace our own aloneness, we will simply use the other as a shield against isolation. Only when one can live like the eagle—with no audience whatsoever—can one turn to another in love; only then is one able to care about the enlargement of the other's being.* (Irvin D. Yalom, *When Nietzsche Wept*)

Let's now do our little quiz. How would you score yourself on a scale of 1-10 with respect to *prioritizing your life*? Do you get out of balance quite readily? Do you have *brownouts*? Are there just too many things to do everyday, and it's terribly frustrating that you are not able to accomplish everything you want to do, or need to do daily? If you score on the low end of the scale, you are need of some true soul-searching. If you score high on the scale, consider yourself quite fortunate, truly blessed, for you are in the minority. The majority of people would say they are *drowning in too many things to do and do not have enough time to accomplish them all.* Choose to focus on those things that are important, fundamentally and foundationally, relationships. The key is discerning, discovering what the important truly is.

Let me invite you to enter my next chapter, *principle #6* on the *power of embracing mutual trust.* I am confident it will help you in this journey. Thus, in summary, choose to internalize, prioritize, and operationalize the following insight. It will inspire you to re-program and re-prioritize your life.

> *You must give birth to your images.*
> *Fear not the strangeness you feel.*
> *The future must enter you.*
> *Long before it happens.*

> — Rainer Maria Rilke

6

EMBRACE MUTUAL TRUST, RESPONSIBILITY, AND ACCOUNTABILITY

You may be deceived if you trust too much, but you will live in torment if you do not trust enough.

— Frank Crane

When my daughter, Jessica, had completed her junior year in high school, like many families, we started the process of visiting colleges. Now, that summer, we must have been on a dozen campuses, exploring various options with Jessica; how far should the college be from our hometown of Leesburg, Virginia; what majors were available, what was the college's culture? Needless to say, with so many different trips, there were more than just a few interesting moments. Noteworthy among them was one at a school (unnamed): during a tour of the dormitory, we observed a young man walking down the hallway with only a towel wrapped around him. Obviously, this was a coed dorm, housing both young men and women, but this scene caused an immediate "flap" with my daughter. Thus, that particular tour was truncated, and we left the campus somewhat abruptly. It was quite clear that my daughter, who loves her privacy, did not want to go to a college with men and women sharing the same dorms.

By the end of that summer, she had narrowed her choices to four schools. Her mom and I thought that was fine, and encouraged her to apply to all four; and, if she was really certain with her choice, to make an appropriate deposit to reserve a space in the dormitory. Thus, she applied to all four, was accepted to all four, and made room deposits, with Dad's money, to all four schools. That was fine for awhile, until the time came for her to make a final decision, and withdraw her deposits from three of the four colleges.

She asked her mom and me to help her make her final decision. We said, "No." That was her choice, and we trusted that she would make an intelligent decision. As we told Jessica, free choice *is the greatest gift God gives us, and this will be one of your biggest.* She wasn't really comfortable with this advice; in fact, she was quite annoyed with her parents, but sometime between Thanksgiving and Christmas, Jessica did make her decision, and the other deposits were withdrawn.

So Jessica finished her senior year, graduating that May, and started to prepare for her college career. Toward the end of the summer, the time came for us to drive Jessica down to her college. And she told me, "Dad, when you drop me off at College, *don't cry."* Now, Jessica is a big hit in our family. She's our only daughter. We have one son. I am one of four boys, with three brothers. I have four nephews, no nieces. My wife is an only child. Her parents were single children in their families. Thus, I think you would agree; Jessica, the only female in both sides of the family, is a big hit, and very special to us.

Now, Jessica was raised as an Episcopal, but had attended a pretty good Catholic prep school. She chose to attend a Baptist-affiliated college in East Tennessee, Carson-Newman. And, if this wasn't enough of an interesting twist, Jessica had really never been away from home, except for short, one or two-week summer camp visits. This college was located some 460 miles from Leesburg.

I believe it was around the 20th of August of 1992 that we drove Jessica down to Carson-Newman. And, after being there for three or four days, getting her furniture, school books, attending all of the orientation sessions, it was time to leave; time to return to Leesburg. And what do I remember? "Dad, when you leave me, *don't cry."*

The moment had arrived. We were leaving. Her then, ten-year old brother, had very little interest in this entire process and was in the backseat asleep. It was around midday; we were standing on the big beautiful porch of her dormitory. Her Mom said goodby, then hugged and kissed her, and headed off toward the car. It was my time and what do I remember? *Don't cry.* I hugged and kissed Jess, telling her how proud we were of her. I told her she could always call on us for any support. And I told her that I loved her and that she was very special in our lives. Then, I walked off the porch, headed to the car, to begin the trip back to Leesburg. But I *didn't cry.*

Barbara and I drove to Roanoke, which is about halfway home, some four hours from Carson-Newman College. We couldn't talk. We didn't talk. I stopped the car in Roanoke and called Jessica. Now why did I do that? Well, it had been some four hours. I had had time to reflect that one of the men's dorms was quite close to her dorm, and time to suspect there were guys up there, with binoculars, looking through the blinds at my daughter, preying on my daughter—predators with hormones out of control. But what could I do at that point? I could pray, could choose not to think about the vulnerabilities of my daughter with that band of sex-crazed fanatics. *Or, I could trust and trust unconditionally.* I chose the latter. Could I "sorta trust"? No, I don't know how to do that. You either trust, or you distrust, and there is nothing in between. My daughter and I stayed in touch, virtually every day, during her four years at Carson-Newman, the first three years by telephone, the last year on the Internet. (It was a lot less costly.) She graduated in 1996, is now married to a terrific young man, and they are the proud parents of our beautiful 1-year old granddaughter, Caroline.

People say that trust is essential in business, because controlling people is very expensive. So they seek trust first, and hope to build sensitivity to one another later. This is backward. Trust can only arise when people have deep, intense interest in each other. You don't just look at the nice and pleasant aspects of that entity. You look for all you can see, until that person becomes part of your life.
(Miha Pogacnik)

Another "signature" story that applies to the issue of trust and trust-worthiness is the one regarding a student pilot and their instructor. When a student flies for the first time by themselves, this is called a "solo." Now, the last flight before solo, there is an Instructor Pilot (IP) with you, either to your left, your right, behind, or in front of you, somewhere in the platform. The IP may have a hood over their head, their hands in their lap, but there is a *state* that the IP is in during that last flight before solo. What is that *state* called? Think. It's called *being there.* Now, at solo, which is typically the next morning or afternoon, depending on the weather, there is another *state* that the IP is in. What is that called? It's called *not there*. It's not, gee, I wish I were there. No, it's called *not there*. It's a lot like trusting my daughter at college. You either trust and trust unconditionally, or you distrust. There is nothing in between. And trust is not an emotion, a feeling; it is a behavior. And, without it, relationships become mere transactions.

Let me share with my readers another "signature" story about an incident with my son, Andrew. He had graduated from the eighth grade (middle school) and was entering high school, which started in the ninth. Now, as you might imagine the cultures are a bit different between a middle school (grades 6-8) and high school (grades 9-12). So, it was the latter part of August of 1997 and my son was entering a good prep school in Middleburg, Virginia. I remember vividly that first morning. I had driven him to school, arriving on schedule about 8:00 a.m. We pulled up in front, having driven though the parking lot, witnessing many of the kids parking their cars and walking into the school. Needless to say, the young women, dressed quite differently and obviously were a lot more mature than the ones Andrew had been used to in middle school. We sat there for a moment, with Andrew surveying the scene and observing the young women. He said, rather matter of factly, "Dad, I think this is going to work."

As a responsible father, at that moment, this caused quite a bit of concern for me. I then leaned over to give my son a big hug and wish him well on his first day of school, and he jumped back in apparent embarassment. Dad, "You don't have to give me a hug every morning anymore." I knew then that life as I had known it was over. My son, who was almost fifteen years old, but six foot tall at that point, and a very handsome young man (takes after his mom) had apparently other things on his mind. This was a "bodacious" paradigm shift. But, again, what could I do about it? Right. Nothing but, pray and TRUST. Again, not almost trust, but trust my son to be responsible and accountable with the choices he would be making at his new school. And, wow, did I ever really need a hug that morning. But, a new chapter had opened for my son, and the normal hug that I had been so accustomed to was no longer required. Andrew loved Notre Dame Academy, had a great time, and graduated some four years later. He is now entering his junior year at his college in Rhode Island.

I attended a Leadership Conference a couple of years ago, and on the agenda, was a Senior Executive with Nordstrom Corporation the terrific Seattle-based upscale apparel store. He spoke about the culture that Nord-strom believes in, and nurtures everyday, as their "guests" are welcomed into their stores all over the country. It was a fascinating presentation. He said they are very careful about whom they invite to join their organization; their teams, which I already knew. In fact, I understand that interviews for their sales force, which are, by far, the most critically important positions, might take several days to complete. These individuals are their ambassadors and fulfill the most important function in all of Nordstrom. For they *Touch the Customer.* Their Office of Human Resources also is quite aggressive at checking references and routinely administers a battery of test instruments to assess the integrity and honesty of each applicant.

The speaker said that if an applicant had ever been in sales, that really is not an important factor in their decision to offer employment or not. What really impressed me was what he then said; their bottom line, their agenda, is to hire only *"nice people,"* people who truly love the merchandising career field, and who want to build a professional career with Nordstrom. These are people who do not easily become annoyed with others relying on them for service. I thought mentioning the word "nice" was amazing. It's something that all of us know, all of us put a great deal of emphasis on in our relationships. But he said what everyone already knows, yet is reluctant to say. It was so simple, yet so profound. The speaker said, you could have a terrific record in sales, but, if in the judgment of the interviewers, you did not seem to be a "nice" person, emotionally balanced, you would not be asked to join their team. He said, to Nordstrom, a "nice" person is one who truly connects with others. Such a person has those innate skills to just put people at ease, to help create a pleasant shopping experience for all guests.

> *The greatest need in the human body is oxygen. The greatest need in the human soul is just to be understood; just to be affirmed as a human being.* (Stephen Covey)

The sales force at Nordstrom respect themselves, and they respect and treat others with great dignity, people who are different from them, who are of a different race, color, gender, religion, or age. The employees of Nordstrom are given space, freedom. These are people who invest in relationships, for they know relationships are all there is.

Chances are you have heard of a very real and remarkable incident that happened at one of Nordstrom's stores. Someone actually provided a refund for a set of automobile tires. Now, Nordstrom, at least at the time of this writing, does not sell automobile tires. However, at Nordstrom, the individuals who warmly "host" and serve their customers, are told, and they really believe, they have the authority and freedom to use good judgment on the floor. They are repeatedly advised, and they really believe, it is easier to get forgiveness than permission. How much, in free advertisng, has Nordstrom received from that incident? Would you believe hundreds of thousands of dollars? In the Nordstrom culture, employees have a bias to first say, "Sure, we can do that." For it is a high-trust culture that brings together idealism and pragmatism. Saying you must provide customer satisfaction is not good enough at Nordstrom. They are committed to consistently exceeding customer expectations at that crucial moment; that one chance they have to WOW their guests, their external customers.

The Nordstrom executive said they are not in the transaction business. They create "moments of truth" for their guests. Nordstrom believes you "live or die" with repeat business. And you do not just satisfy your customers. You must exceed their expectations of both the service delivered and the quality of the merchandise purchased. And, obviously, they must be willing to pay a little more money for the merchandise. And, they will and do if they feel valued and believe the merchandise is of true quality, which it is. Nordstrom's focus, their philosophy, is to create a partnership with their guests, to invest heavily in relationships. And, apparently, they do quite well.

> *Things themselves do not have intrinsic properties. All the properties flow from their relationships. This is what I mean by understanding the properties of the parts from the dynamics of the whole, because these relationships are dynamic relationships. So the only way to understand the part is to understand its relationship to the whole. This insight occurred in physics in the 1920s and this is also a key insight of ecology. Ecologists think exactly in this way. They say an organism is defined by its relationship to the rest.*
> (Capra Rast, *Belonging in the Universe*)

Another "signature" story which comes readily to mind is the incident I experienced a few years ago with a Corporate Executive Officer (CEO) of a Northern Virginia computer software firm. He called me on the phone, and said, "He had heard about me and wanted me to come by, have a cup of coffee with him, and discuss a rather serious problem he was having with his employees." I was curious and said, "Fine," and went to meet with him. His secretary escorted me into his office, and he was quite cordial, initially.

He then spoke about a corporate retreat his firm had scheduled, and said he needed a facilitator who could help his employees with "communication skills." I thought that was a bit odd, since communication is virtually effortless when there is a deep, enduring trust culture in the organization, but I was willing to listen. The gentleman's voice started to rise a bit, and he became progressively more and more animated and agitated. He said, "There was a communications problem in his company; nobody really talks to anyone around here." At that point, he mentioned that his "door was always open" yet "nobody ever came in the damn door without being defensive. It was hard getting people to open up to each other." He then said, "My management team just doesn't seem to work together well. I don't know if it is jealousy or what the heck is going on there, but the team just doesn't work that well. I have done everything I can think of to get these guys to work together, but to no success." At this point, he was literally screaming in frustration. He said this situation must change, and he wanted it to change during the retreat. He said, "We move really quick around here, and we can whip this baby out in a few days."

By this time in the discussion, he was quite exercised and seemed very confused as to why this communications problem existed in his firm, yet seemed to be very proud of his successful management skills, the success of his firm, and his ability to meet any challenge. After he had presented the issue, and his proposal, I said, "Let me be candid with you. I think I know the problem." Quite taken aback by this, he said, "What? What do you mean? You think you know the problem?" I said, "People don't like you." And, not surprisingly, he didn't like that. I told him that the behavior he had described within his company reflected a toxic, fatiguing, constipating culture that denies individuals' freedoms, freedom to be creative and imaginative, freedom to take ownership of the collective journey they were on. I advised him that, in my view, his firm seem to be hemorrhaging, and he might not realize how serious this issue had become, but, given today's climate of brutal, global competition, he had just described an organization that might be a former organization pretty soon.

While choosing my words in a very diplomatic manner, I told him that he was intimidating, and, very predictably, his employees felt very uncomfortable in expressing themselves to him. His employees feared some type of retribution or negative reaction to decisions they might make, or views that they might have in the firm. I advised him that he must choose to modify or alter his behavior to a less intimidating and menacing style. Typically, in these types of organizational situations, truly "high performers" leave; they take their skills elsewhere. And those who choose to stay, a collection of "mediocrities," either feel there are no alternatives, or they do not have the courage to seek employment elsewhere. These individuals will just produce enough "kinetic" energy in their jobs not to get fired. They become *minimalists.*

Well, our nice coffee chat, at that point, seemed to be coming to a rather uncomfortable conclusion. Needless to say, as my analysis was shared, I perceived the invitation for me to help him out had started to "cool." Thus, we essentially agreed to disagree. While I could, I suppose, have been less candid in my analysis and spoke with some optimism, I just concluded that it was too late. The "boat had take on too much water; the sinking of the boat was accelerating and could not be stopped." I told him his words should reflect his beliefs; and his beliefs, his behavior. As you might imagine, I concluded this organizational culture was too corrosive. I chose not to facilitate their corporate retreat, and never really followed up on their their business success. Clearly, this individual, this organization was in mis-alignment, truly dysfunctional. There existed a virtual vacuum of trust and honesty. The gentleman did not truly care about these people he had recruited, ostensibly because they were talented, knowledgeable, skillful, and available. He saw them only as "things, employees;" cogs in a big mechanical machine, not as human beings with psychological, social, and spiritual needs. This is certainly not being principle-based. We create and choose to embrace internally persuasive excuses and rationalizations to fool our consciences. Among the most potent are these:

- *Everyone does it.* Sorry, my friend, You are deceiving yourself. They don't. "To escape shame and self-contempt, we must learn to deceive ourselves. These lies create a formidable obstacle to action on behalf of truth, and one of the greatest human accomplishments is to find a way to shatter those lies" (Immanuel Kant).

- *To succeed today in business, one has to be a "hard, tough taskmaster," for performance and productivity is everything today.* People who still believe this are cowards and don't read; and, if you don't read today, you might as well not have the ability to read.

- *These people just don't understand.* No, you don't understand. "Seek first to understand, before you seek to be understood" (Stephen Covey).

- *People just don't respect their bosses today.* It is not through authority that one acquires greatness today, but through influence. People who hold on to "power" really don't have it. They just think they do. Powerful people give it away; and if you abuse it, it is taken from you.

- *I have no time for principle-based subtleties.* Is that right? Try unemployment, abject failure, "toxic relationships," disillusionment, severe depression, or divorce.

- *Relying on principles to guide my life is a luxury I cannot afford right now.* Is that right? Well, your choice is to miss out on this wonderful, joyous human experience; a gift from God, which not one of us asked for, for it is truly a present.

You cannot learn too soon that the most useful thing about principle is that it can always be sacrificed to expediency. (Somerset Maugham)

Implicit in theories impacting the needs of all humans is the notion of caring for and respecting others. In many cases, this caring requires us to forego personal benefits or to bear personal burdens; some level of self-sacrifice is essential to consistent principle-based living. Violating this principle causes one to become selfish in their motives and intentions. Selfishness typically comes in three major forms:

- *Self-Indulgence*: Perhaps the most common and easily identifiable source of un-principled conduct, this trait is associated with people who often coverup the selfish motive with noble sounding sentiments, for example, "I'm doing it for the company."

- *Self-Protection*: Involves blameshifting, an unwillingness to accept the consequences of prior behavior. "The Devil made me do it." (You cannot be committed to living a principle-based life and talk yourself out of a problem you have behaved yourself into.)

- *Self-Righteousness*: "Only I am enlightened. If only everyone would just see things the way I do." The challenge one confronts with this viewpoint arises when chosen beliefs are at variance with the honest, good faith views of others who have at least an equal right to particpate in the decision-making process.

One must be truthful to themselves first and only then will they be truthful to others. Edward R. Murrow, the legendary journalist, said," *To be persuasive, we must be believable; To be believable, we must be credible; To be credible, we must be truthful.* A terrific little story captures the fundamental issue regarding words, beliefs, and actions. Let me share it with you.

Love

Newspaper columnist and minister George Crane tells of a wife who came into his office full of hatred toward her husband. "I do not only want to get rid of him, I want to get even. Before I divorce him, I want to hurt him as much as he has hurt me."

Dr. Crane suggested an ingenious plan. "Go home and act as if you really loved your husband. Tell him how much he means to you. Praise him for every decent trait. Go out of your way to be as kind, considerate, and generous as possible. Spare no efforts to please him, to enjoy him. Make him believe you love him. After you've convinced him of your undying love and that you cannot live without him, then drop the bomb. Tell him that you're getting a divorce. That will really hurt him."

With revenge in her eyes, she smiled and exclaimed, "Beautiful, beautiful. Will he ever be surprised!" And she did it with enthusiasm, acting "as if." For two months she showed love, kindness, listening, giving, reinforcing, sharing. When she didn't return, Crane called. "Are you ready now to go through with the divorce?" "Divorce?" she exclaimed, "Never! I discovered I really do love him." Her actions had changed her feelings. Motion resulted in emotion. The ability to love is established not so much by fervent promise as by often repeated deeds. (J. Allan Petersen, *The Myth of the Greener Grass*)

The corporate executive who realized his management team was so dysfunctional could not see what, to everyone else, was so obvious. Could you choose to change his behavior? Of course, he could but it is not easy. In a way, it's like an alcoholic, who has to virtually "hit bottom" before they realize their illness will eventually result in a family breaking up, careers aborted, and experience a deteriorating physical body.

During my meeting with the CEO of the computer software firm, I thought of Peter Senge's insightful description of the "management team myth," which he addressed in his terrific book, *The Fifth Discipline*. It was included among his seven learning disabilities that he has observed in organizations.

> *All too often, teams in business spend their time fighting for turf, avoiding anything that will make them look bad personally, and pretending that everyone is behind the team's collective strategy— maintaining the appearance of a cohesive team. To keep up the image, they seek to squelch disagreement; people with serious reservations avoid stating them publicly, and joint decisions are watered-down compromises reflecting what everyone can live with, or else reflecting one person's view foisted on the group. If there is disagreement, it's usually expressed in a manner that lays blame, polarizes opinion, and fails to reveal the underlying differences in assumptions and experience in a way that the team as a whole could learn.* (Peter Senge)

So, what leadership trait/quality was missing from their chief executive? The gentleman was obviously out of balance, out of alignment. I suspect he was one of those individuals who believe they "know it all." They "learned that" and are *just not willing, or they are not able, to unlearn and relearn*, which is crucially important today if one is to continue to grow. The executive's behavior also reflected someone who doesn't read very much, who is unfamiliar with current literature on management/leadership skills. For if he did, he would certainly know that without a deep, enduring trust culture, it is currently problematic his firm will survive; years ago maybe, but not today. Effective servant leadership rests on a foundation of mutual trust. Without it, you have very little chance to survive as an organization.

It's my view that while we do talk about trust, we have very little trust experience at a deep level. But, this character and behavioral trait is very important. According to Gordon Shea, trust is not an abstract, theoretical, idealistic goal forever beyond our reach. He describes it as the "miracle ingredient in life—a lubricant that reduces friction, a bonding agent that glues together disparate parts, a catalyst that facilitates action. No substitute—neither present nor promise—will do the job as well." Unconditional trust, a clear expression of faith, enhances significantly security, reduces inhibitions and defensiveness, and allows you to share, to truly connect with feelings and dreams. To be an individual of true alignment is to have a kind of openness to the world and to relationships, an ability to trust uncertain things beyond your control. Being human means accepting promises from other people and trusting that others will keep those promises. A fulfilled life is not possible when one no longer trusts other humans and no longer chooses to engage or nurture ties to the human community. One cannot acquire trust; it can only be given and given freely to someone who is trustworthy. To trust permits you to put your deepest fears in the palms of the hands of others, knowing that it will be treated with care, because the relationships become more important than you are.

It is clear to me that new theories and approaches are needed in the field of organizational psychology regarding how we examine the nature of trust, how we must re-define work, and how we craft employment contracts. Particularly important is the need to explore the dynamics of trust in relationships. While one can find numerous definitions of *trust*, I think *an assured reliance on the character or truth of someone* works pretty well for me. A review of the literature on trust is quite insightful. We have a *biological need* for trust. When we enter this world, trust is a necessity. At birth, we are vulnerable, exposed, and at risk, dependent on others for our survival. And, as we grow older, this need does not go away. We have a *socio-psychological need* for trust. When there is respect and confidence in relationships, when we treat each other with great dignity, even when we are experiencing turbulence in our lives or in our organizations, there will be open communication, providing a level of emotional well-being.

As humans, we have an *emotional need* for trust, a measure of how we feel about ourselves. We seek a feeling of self-respect, centeredness, self-worth, balance, and alignment in our lives. We have a *relationship need* for trust; and, even though we tend to act often to the contrary, we do not live independent of our relationships. And how do we create *self-trust?* We do this by respecting ourselves, by accepting both responsibility and account-ability for our behavior, treating others with honor and dignity, and adhering to a personal code of moral values. And, at a deeper level, with respect to accountability, M. Scott Peck, in his terrific journey toward spiritual growth, explored this issue in *Further Along the Road Less Traveled.* Dr. Peck spoke of many people who misinterpret the teachings of Jesus Christ and of *judging others. Jesus said, "Judge not, and you will not be judged"; He didn't say, "Never judge." But, each time you judge, be prepared for judgment yourself.* What he was saying was, before you judge anyone else, you must judge yourself, that is, hold yourself accountable. According to William Creed and Richard Miles, there are three different facets of trust:

- *Process-based*: Personal experience of recurring exchanges which create ongoing expectations and norms of obligation about what is felt to be fair treatment;

- *Characteristic-based*: Beliefs about another's trustworthiness that results from a perception of their expertise, intentions, actions, words, and general qualities; and

- *Institutional-based*: Trust in the integrity and competence of informal societal structures.

All three facets are under scrutiny today, and mistrust is highly evident in many organizations—the news media, senior government and corporate leaders, even in the workplace today—in many instances, it's "us against them." But the challenge today is that organizations are asking "employees" to trust while organizations are undergoing real transition at the very time that the nature of employee trust is itself in transition.

Thus, the changing nature of work is a driving factor in any discussion of personal and professional development. Stability, in the form of a job-for-life in any organization, is clearly a relic of the past. Separation is often sudden and unanticipated, dampening any loyalty that might exist. Thus, we must re-define the word "loyalty" and restructure psychological contracts, the unwritten reciprocal relationships between employees and organizations. I suggest we must approach this new terrain with the positive outlook of seeking a life balance that has been largely absent in many of our lives. Charles Handy believes *work must now be viewed in much more of a portfolio sense, shifting frequently and intermittently between varied dimensions of paid work and free work.* We have entered an era of *contingent loyalty;* when people affiliate with high-performing organizations, they will receive *ingredients* for career growth—emotional, spiritual, and financial. Today's stakeholder is seeking organizations that are truly committed to excellence, led by visionaries who invest in the shared purpose of continued education; lifelong learning and training; and human and skills development for everyone, not just the more visible executives.

But I have observed that we too frequently have *contingent loyalty*, and *transactional relationships,* that are commonly found in organizations which are hemorrhaging. You must either avoid these organizations or choose to transform them and transform them from within. If this sounds like "living on the edge" at times, you may want to just get used to it. *Walking the highwire is living. Everything else is waiting (The Great Wallenda).*

An organization's culture refers to its depth of trustworthiness among its stakeholders, the values, beliefs, traditions, operating style, and internal work environment, essentially how things are done. Beliefs and practices that become embedded in an organization's culture can originate anywhere: from one influential individual, work group/team, department, or division; from the bottom of the organizational hierarchy; or from the top. Sometimes, elements of the culture begin with the company's vision, mission statement, or its strategic philosophy. Over time, this cultural foundation becomes "hardened," spreading throughout the organization, affecting long-term employees as well as new hires.

Now, changing toxic cultures is very difficult because of the heavy baggage of deeply held policies, habits, and the emotional clinging of people to the old and familiar. Sometimes senior leaders/managers in organizations succeed in changing the habits and behaviors of small groups of "mid-level" people and even whole departments or divisions, only to find the changes eroding over time by the actions of the rest of the organization. What is communicated, praised, supported, and penalized by the entrenched majority quite often undermines the new emergent culture and halts its progress. *Executives can revamp formal organization charts, move boxes around which, in my opinion, speaks volumes about how and why ineffective communication and a culture of distrust can be so fatiguing and constipating.* They can announce new strategies, bring in managers from the outside, introduce new technologies, open new plants, yet fail to change dysfunctional cultural traits and behaviors because of skepticism about the new directions and covert resistance to them.

What are the costs of "managing employees"? What are the costs of "supervising people"? I suggest today the costs are staggering. Good people leave, taking important skills, competencies and client knowledge with them; they can voice their discontent, thereby hurting morale; use every possible "sick day"; consistently show up late; become apathetic; perform at the minimal acceptable level of productivity—just enough not to be fired. How can you have a commitment to excellence, creativity, and imagination with someone treating you like they own you, controlling you, denying you your dignity? Control is an illusion. In high performing organizations today, people choose to control themselves. There are a number of separate stages of stakeholder involvement/affiliation with their "employers": among them are apathetic workers, disgruntled workers, obedient workers, motivated workers, compliant workers, loyal workers; then committed workers. Today, if an organization does not have true, committed employees, odds are they are a failing, bankrupt organization.

It's simple.... We either get used to thinking about the subtle processes of learning and sharing knowledge in dispersed transient networks ... or we perish. (Tom Peters)

To eliminate old functional mind-sets, there must be a collaborative, collegial culture which fosters a collective sense of both responsibility and accountability among all stakeholders. Traditional organizational hierarchies have become obsolete. They are now recognized as a liability where customer preferences are shifting from standardized products to custom orders and special features, product life cycles are growing shorter, custom mass-production methods are replacing standardization mass production techniques, both internal and external customers are demanding to be treated with respect as individuals, the pace of technological change is accelerating, and market conditions are fluid. These "tired," exploitive, manipulating, stifling hierarchical models no longer can deliver responsible customer service or adapt fast enough to changing conditions. There is not only acceptance now, but virtually total reliance upon decentralized decision making which shortens response times and spurs new ideas, creative thinking, innovation, and greater commitment and ownership on the part of all stakeholders. I believe that a different conversation is necessary in organizations truly committed to excellence; not just alternating monologues but a dialogue that helps us connect to one another and learn more about how we each see the world. For this to happen, genuine and empathic listening and the creation of deep enduring trust cultures in relationships must occur. For in its absence, we will inherently become "bogged down" in corrosive, literally self-destructive relationships. (And ALL organizations are nothing but interconnected relationships.)

It's my sense that the operative organizational paradigm of the future will be not unlike a movie set, where technicians, caterers, designers, actors, directors, producers, logisticians, writers, specialists of all types, come together for a definite period of time, some for just a few days, some for 4 or 5 weeks, others for a bit longer. They are introduced to each other, and after they contribute their particular expertise/service, they then might leave, be replaced, then their replacements may leave, go to another movie set, to provide their particular expertise/creativity. And, as these cycles are played out, the contributors are going to have multiple revenue streams, simultaneously. That will be the operative model. And what will be truly interesting is that these individuals may or may not have previously known each other, or certainly, not know each other very well. But, what they have in common is their passion, their creativity, their innovativeness, their imagination, to pursue excellence in their professions. *Leadership does not reside solely in individuals.*

> *Leadership resides in the culture and is everywhere, or it is nowhere.* (Peter Senge)

Rather than focus on structures and plans in organizations, we need to focus more on the process by which we create our plans, our intentions. Dr. Margaret Wheatley, in her insightful exploration of *Leadership and the New Science*, states that "we need to see these plans, standards, organization charts, not as objects that we complete, but as processes that enable a group to keep clarifying its intent and strengthening its connections to new people and new information. It is believed we should pay less reverence for the objects that are created, and much more attention to the processes we use to create them." Healthy processes create and nurture better relationships among all people, more meaning in who we are and more insight into what our life is about and what is going on around us. And "with these new insights, we develop greater capacity to know what to do, weaving together an organization as resilient and flexible as a spider's web." Thus, as we learn to live better together, respecting our differences, respecting our uniqueness, we are genuinely rewarded in our behavior. We become more gentle, more civil, more decent, more understanding, more patient, more serving, celebrating life's gift. And this gift, which we did not ask for, we even feel we are not deserving of, brings greater riches, greater life fulfillment, emotionally and spiritually.

> *Life is change. Growth is optional. Choose wisely.* (Karen Kaiser Clark)

In the accelerating, dynamic, fast-changing global business environments of today, the capacity to introduce new strategies and approaches—approaches that nurture the conditions where all individuals heavily invest in the creative learning process—relies heavily on failure for failure, along with doubt, ambiguity and uncertainty, is a friend of, and an important part of, the iterative process of creativity. *One doesn't just jump on a bicycle for the very first time and ride it successfully. It just doesn't happen.* And human creativity, which happens when one gives up their sense of self is vital today if a company or organization is not only to perform effectively over an extended period of time, but to survive. And this action; this organizational form, must materialize from the *inside-out.* Imposing, directing, demanding from the *outside-in* is rarely effective. To that end, strategic agility and speed in responding to new conditions require a culture that quickly creates, accepts, and supports efforts to adapt to environmental change, rather than a culture that has to be coaxed or encouraged to change. There is a new business axiom that is alive and well today. It's "you've got to be quick, my friend—or you are dead."

> *The illiterate of the future will not be the person who cannot read. It will be the person who does not know how to learn.* (Alvin Toffler)

So, let's do a little test. On a scale 1-10, a score of 1 or 2 suggests you are totally out of alignment. You trust no one. You cannot believe what people tell you. You just know that everyone is out for themselves, selfish individuals out to enhance their own agendas. You disbelieve that people can really become selfless. A high score, 8 or higher, suggests you believe in the power of trust, even trusting unconditionally. You believe we can choose to be extraordinary contributors in our organization, our communities, and in our families, *for the model is the family.*

Let me now invite you to explore *principle #7, the power of valuing and celebrating differences.* For celebrating true diversity, and not just cultural, religious, racial differences, but diverse opinions as well, does not weaken, but strengthens us all.

7

VALUE AND CELEBRATE
DIFFERENCES

Alone we can do so little; together we can do so much.

— Helen Keller

Mother Teresa shared this insight, "If you judge people, you have no time to love them." What she was referring and alerting us to is a natural inclination—which should be resisted—to seek comfort and connect with just those that make us feel comfortable; made us feel like we were the same. Well, my friends, "sameness" weakens all of us, personally as well as organizationally. If you do not choose to see the power that one derives from working with, collaborating with, and cooperating with people who are different from you, it is quite problematic that you will even get close to your highest level of potential in life. Certainly, your organization will not. For, it is only through valuing and celebrating differences—the uniqueness and marvelous gifts of all people who lift the spirits and enhance the possibility of one becoming a far more effective person—that one can live a truly self-fulfilled life.

What is meant generally by the term diversity? I believe it must capture inclusiveness; a mosaic of people who bring a variety of backgrounds, styles, perspectives, values, and beliefs as assets to the groups and organizations with which they interact. As a mosaic, it clearly is not the traditional "melting pot" of cultural differences. A mosaic allows people to retain their individuality while they contribute collectively to the larger community. This definition of diversity includes everyone, and it is the one thing we all have in common. All six and a half billion of us on this earth are unique; no two of us alike. And isn't it a marvelous blessing that nobody on this earth sees the world exactly the same as you do, or I do? It is no more complicated than different people really doing things differently. Irrespective of how hard we work at understanding others, we fall short consistently of adequately representing or understanding anyone else. We have all experienced discussing events that occur in our lives—movies we might have seen, a national calamity we may have witnessed, speeches we may have heard on television—but, upon asking others what they thought, we get as many interpretations as there are people we asked.

> *Diversity creates one and only one thing: Opportunity. Business, in the mad global marketplace, needs a rush of serious creativity. Creativity is, invariably, a byproduct of sparks, new views, juxtaposed interests. How does a company acquire those assets? Diversity!* (Tom Peters)

Although culture—a rather complex concept, which captures a system of beliefs, behavioral norms, mores, customs, and values—is certainly a relevant issue in our lives today, my *principle of celebrating differences* goes far beyond just essentially recognizing the value in respecting another's shared history and identity. While culture may be the most defining characteristic of an individual or group, we are often unaware of its true power and influence, particularly when we are surrounded by individuals who look like us, act like us, think like us. In these cases, culture is virtually invisible. We don't see it, or feel it.

Similar to a painting with sharp contrasts drawing our attention to the differences in color, form, structure, so does a multicultural society lead us to notice the aspects of culture which most dramatically make up our identity and social practices. However, culture should be thought of in a broader manner, not solely in terms of nationality and ethnicity. Just recognizing and tolerating multicultural diversity remains a rather immature posture if we are to truly pursue and acquire greatness in our lives. We must not fear, but seek out *differences*, then choose to open our vulnerabilities to being influenced by them. Respect and relate to *differences* not solely with our eyes and ears, but with our hearts as well.

Reserve judgment, *ask people for their unique perspectives and listen to them carefully, empathically, which always brings us closer together.* Actively listen for differences. We may or may not agree with them, or approve or disapprove of their behavior. We may or may not even take a position. But choose to value, to celebrate these unique perspectives, these views, which creates an exciting and rich mosaic and tapestry of interpretations of life. For only by choosing to join together can we create and embrace the changes we both desire.

We have a choice; we can continue to fear "differences" and rely on "sameness" or similarities, which clearly will weaken us all, or we can pursue and celebrate "differences," which will take us to new heights of greatness in our lives and in our organizations.

There is a powerful paradox at work with sharing meaning in differences and diversity. If we are willing to listen eagerly for diverse interpretations, we discover that our differing perceptions somehow originate from a unifying center. We don't have to agree with each other in order to think well together. There is no need for us to be joined at the head. We are joined already by our human hearts. (Margaret Wheatley)

However, cultural, gender, racial, and ethnic diversity still means different things to different people. Some people believe that diversity is about quotas, compliance with the law, and affirmative action. These are antiquated and obsolete definitions. Others believe that diversity is something that will happen on its own without intervention. However, I don't believe the valuing and celebrating of diversity should be left up to chance. It is important that organizations take action to encourage and foster diversity in the workplace, for differences strengthen us. All of us are more important than any one of us. And creating a "Diversity Management or Training Program" is not the answer. Acceptance of and deeply valuing differences cannot be dictated. You have to truly believe in the power of "differences"; it has to be in your DNA, an innate belief, oozing out of your pores. Valuing and celebrating differences will create and nurture a culture that will provide a broad range of ideas, allowing easy adaptation to major changes, an inclusiveness, an openness, freely expressed, from everyone. Life depends upon and truly relies on differences to bring diverse interpretations of events/decisions/activities, which are absolutely vital for humans as well as organizations if they are to continue to grow and prosper. If a system or organization becomes too homogenous, relying on "sameness," it becomes extremely vulnerable to environmental shifts, resulting in resistance to change/creativity/innovation. Today, if one group is dominant, the entire system/organization invites increased risk and possible dysfunction or stagnation; thus failure.

The importance and power of differences in our lives is prophetically shared by Gary Snyder in a verse from his 1960's poem, *Turtle Island:*

> *In the next century ... or the one after that, they say, are valleys and pastures. We can meet there in peace if we make it. To climb these coming crests one word to you, to you and your children: Stay together. Learn the flowers. Go light.*

To me, the key words are "learn the flowers." Seek out, cherish, celebrate the uniqueness of differences in all relationships. It becomes a spiritual awakening, and joyously represents nature's beauty. It is suggested that you not only open your eyes, but open your mind, open your heart. Realize that it is truly impossible to explore the natural world and find a separated individual. Think interdependently; recognize that while independence, the "I don't need you—I can do this myself" attitude, might be a political concept, there is no evidence that it is found in biology. To pursue and acquire alignment in our lives, we need to come together in dialogue, in conversations; we need to interact with each other. For only in relationships; relationships centered and anchored around and within a shared sense of purpose, with many types of individuals, can we truly discover who we are, that *fire within*—and what our life is about. Albeit, while we have achieved remarkable success in many fields, the way we have historically created "balkanized," repressive human organizations, which have, as a foundation, relied upon *human distrust,* has divided us, and hindered creativity and human imagination. For anyone who reads today and stays reasonably current in the literature of human and organizational behavior, realizes that today's workplace requires different competencies, skills, different paradigms of thinking, if one is to have any chance at all to embrace the dizzying pace of change and find true meaning and purpose in our lives.

The idea of using "power and control over" language, creating "managers," "bosses," "employees," "labor," "supervisors," and "layers," which has relied upon a manipulation and exploitation of human beings, has created and nurtured significant doses of toxicity and distrust ... in organizations. And, *while it served us quite well early in the past century,* today, this model, this "tired" and virtually obsolete language, deservedly lies in the dustpan of history. If this language remains common in your organization today, it is quite problematic that your organization will, in the near future, no longer be found in the yellow pages. And your demise will be well deserved. We must choose to change our language and how we relate to each other. Telling a tulip to flower, and if it doesn't do exactly what you say, you scream at it just doesn't work, does it? It's the same with human beings. We need to invest in, create and nurture the conditions, through committing ourselves to interdependent thought and behavior, which will quite predictably result in "tulips blossoming" and our relationships being strengthened.

> *Find the person who will love you because of your differences and not in spite of them and you have found life's love. Happily, we are all individuals similar to others in many ways and yet very different in others. It is these differences that make us who we are and determine the directions in which we will grow and change. Being normal doesn't mean giving up our uniqueness so that we can be like everyone else. It means being proud of the ways in which we are uniquely us. In fact, it is this aspect of ourselves that attracts others and is our most loving gift to them.* (Leo Buscaglia)

Seek out and listen empathically and very carefully to those who are different than you, especially those who are of a different educational level, different gender, race, ethnicity, skin color, religion, age—or who have different life experiences and who have a different socio-economic status. Avoid the rather immature posture of psychologically competing with others, where colleagues are pitted against each other to improve performance. Competition is healthy, but only competition that resides within each of us, that *fire within* ... where we choose to raise the high bar on our performance every day. Realize that the paradigm extant in today's workplace, the rules, have changed. And respecting, embracing, and celebrating differences, of all types/kinds, is vital to our continued growth as humans, spiritually, emotionally, and certainly intellectually. And, as we choose to grow, the organizations we choose to affiliate with, invest in, and contribute to, are also advanced.

Some of the most pervasive obstacles to valuing and embracing "differences" are the reliance upon, and addiction to, what we have traditionally called the "good old boy's network." It pre-dates 1900, and unfortunately, still exists today in far too many organizational cultures. It has not been any one individual's fault that it exists, but it has been quite perverse. Its foundation rests on a bedrock of ignorance, and it will take considerable knowledge and choosing to think differently just to realize the extent and depth of this ignorance.

> *My continuing passion is to part a curtain, that invisible shadow that falls between people, the veil of indifference to each other's presence, each other's wonder, each other's human plight.* (Eudora Welty)

What could be the root cause of this pathology? Dr. H. Keith Brodie, former President of Duke University, argues that racism, sexism, and religious and cultural intolerance have one thing in common. They are all ways of denying that other people are of the same kind as we are; essentially, some people are viewed as less human than ourselves. Whatever the manifestation and whoever the target may be, group hatred and suspicion arise from a primitive psychological mechanism that has nothing to do with race, color, creed, gender, physical disability, or sexual orientation of the excluded others.

Dr. Brodie suggests that biases may have less to do with outer objective reality, and more to do with inner psychological defense systems. It is also argued that, until fairly recently in our history, educational institutions have not necessarily enlightened our community to attitudes of tolerance and humility. Nor has corporate America voluntarily fought intolerance and inhumanity publicly at every opportunity. However, I believe it is changing quickly and changing for the better. Why? Because we have matured as a people and as a nation. Jesus said, "Love thy neighbor as thyself." He wasn't talking about just "white boys," people you go to church, synagogue, or the mosque with, people that look like you. Jesus wasn't speaking about those people whom we share mutual interests with. He was speaking to a larger issue. All are precious in his sight; all of us have value, and we all share in the same fate. We are truly blessed in the marvelous diversity all around us: differences in appearance, culture, language, socio-economic status, age, religion, gender, race, skin color, sexual orientation, ideas, and ways of thinking. There is significant empirical evidence today that oppression rarely, if ever, occurs between equals. People all over the world and in all organizations, with very few exceptions want the same things;

they want to serve and help others, to be valued, to be recognized and affirmed, and to find meaning in their lives.

We hold these truths to be self-evident; that all men are created equal; that they are endowed by their creator with certain unalienable rights; that among these are life, liberty, and the pursuit of happiness. (U.S. Declaration of Independence)

Differences are about recognizing they are causes of—rather than road blocks to—our organizational success. Valuing and celebrating differences creates an all-inclusive work environment that results in significant benefits, enabling all to develop and reach their full potential. Illustrative of what I am speaking about is a powerful story of an American hero and his understanding of the value and strength found in *differences.*

Joshua Lawrence Chamberlain, a Cvil War hero, who attained the rank of Major General, was elected governor of Maine four times, and served as President of Bowdoin College for 12 years, was a military man of remarkable courage and commitment to serve his country. Little Round Top, an extremely important piece of terrain, at the Battle of Gettysburg, is where Colonel Joshua Chamberlain, the Commander of the 20th Maine Regiment, made history. His acts of bravery and inspirational leadership, not only earned him the Congressional Medal of Honor, our nation's highest military honor, but the singular, notable and heroic achievements of the 20th Maine late in the afternoon of July 2, 1863 turned the tide against the Army of Virginia and led, on the following day, to the famed *Picketts Charge* and the defeat of the Confederate forces, therefore turning the tide against General Lee's Army.

However, I want to share with my readers an incident involving Colonel Chamberlain and his successful attempt to inspire some 150 deserters to join the 20th Maine as they were marching toward Gettysburg for the fateful battle. This incident reportedly occurred some ten days prior to their arrival at the ultimate battlefield. It was compellingly and quite dramatically portrayed in the classic civil war movie *Gettysburg.*

When the 20th Maine Regiment was formed, its strength consisted of about 1000 men. As they approached and prepared for the Gettysburg battle, previous hostilities had cost them over 700 losses. Thus, their strength was less than 300. Colonel Chamberlain strongly believed he could convince the deserters to join his Regiment. He needed them as riflemen, but he also believed in their goodness, even as deserters. He genuinely believed in the value of all human beings. He had taken a leave of absence as a Professor of Rhetoric and Chaplain of Bowdoin College, coming from an entirely different background than the deserters. Yes, they were *different*, but that did not diminish his respect, his deep caring, for these gentlemen. To that end, unlike the guards who had brought them to him, he treated them with great respect and dignity.

He was told he could shoot them. He chose not to. In fact, he told them that he "would not do that." They had been denied food, in an attempt to "break" them, demanding their compliance to rejoin their Union forces. He first ordered the guards to leave and requested food be prepared for them. He then met with their spokesperson, in a powerful moment of genuine dialogue, an open conversation where Colonel Chamberlain reflected deep trust, believing that is the effective lubricant necessary for truly connecting with other humans.

Colonel Chamberlain told the men that they had signed three-year papers and had an obligation to remain in the Army. He said they would be very soon asked to join in an historic struggle, a battle that would likely determine the ultimate winner in the Civil War. And their cause was just. He appealed to their understanding of the larger good, the true purpose of this struggle. This was a war unlike any other in the history of the world. It was not a war over money, or land, or the love of killing. *They were committed to freeing other human beings*. He spoke with great passion and conviction. Colonel Chamberlain told the deserters, if they *chose* to join his Regiment, they would be issued rifles, and nothing ever would be said about their status. And for those who *chose* not to join the Regiment, they would be brought along under guard, and when the battle was over, he would do what he could to help the men.

All but a handful of the men *chose* to join the Regiment; but tragically, very few survived the horrific second day of the Battle of Gettysburg. But their bravery in the face of relentless, repeated Confederate attacks allowed the Union forces to hold this key terrain. Colonel Chamberlain respected these gentlemen. They were initially angry, disillusioned with the perceived incompetence of Union General officers and unwilling to continue their service. It would have been very easy for Colonel Chamberlain to have taken an entirely different approach, one that would not have resulted in their voluntarily joining his Regiment. But his sincerity was real. He deeply cared for these men, and he was passionate in his conviction that their cause was just. But he also said they were there to help each other, to defend each other, for their cause, to free other humans, was just too important to deny. It was truly a powerful moment, reflecting a *win-win mentality*, and capturing the essence of and belief in *strength being inherent in differences.*

> *Unlike diversity, which is the dynamic mosaic of people who bring a variety of cultural backgrounds, styles, beliefs, values, biases, to organizations with which they interact ... differences ... with truly unlimited power and importance ... capture the uniqueness ... the richness ... the talents ... the gifts ... of all humans and cry out for understanding.* (Travis L. Sample)

Even before I left the Air Force, some twelve years ago, I had developed a habit of about every two weeks going to a library, walking through the "stacks," and grabbing about a dozen journals/periodicals, not even looking at the titles. I would find a quiet place to sit down and then, methodically, go through them, looking for and "processing" different topics/themes, different approaches, different areas of interest for whomever contributes to or reads that particular journal. I would normally devote about an hour or hour an half to this exercise. Why did I do this? I believe to be an educated, life-long learner, one has to read "outside the box." You don't have to be a University Professor to seek exposure to areas of study/interest that are new to you. Choose to be curious, curious about issues outside your normal area of expertise. Doing this keeps your mind open and vulnerable to the power of "differences." I suggest you consider this habit, one that is potentially "life changing." Try it a couple of times. I think you will surprised how valuable this experience can be.

> *What you are ... who you are ... is the basis of what you dream and think, accept, and reject, feel, and perceive.* (John Mason Brown)

The time is 1924; the setting is Paris, France and the venue, the Olympic games. In the Oscar-winning movie, *Chariots of Fire*, the famed "flying Scot," Eric Liddell, portrayed by Ben Cross, chooses because of his deep religious beliefs, not to run his event's heats on the Sabbath. Under intense pressure from the Olympic Organizers and Olympic Committee of the United Kingdom, Eric, a Baptist minister and missionary, maintains his principles and resists their pressure to run, pressure even from his future King. They truly could not understand why he felt so strongly about his faith. His powerful faith and Biblical interpretation reflected a clear difference between him and the senior individuals responsible for fielding their outstanding track team, training to compete and win against the world's greatest athletes. One of his teammates, who had won a Silver Medal earlier in the games in the 400-meter hurdles, met with the United Kingdom Olympic Committee and offered to give up his position to compete in the 400 meters race to Eric, which would allow Eric to compete.

That race, to include all heats, was scheduled during the week. Again, the power of differences and synergy provided an alternative opportunity that satisfied and met the needs of all. A momentous event in the movie was the victory by Eric in the 400-meter run. As he was about to cross the finish line, he shared with the viewers the following: *Where does the power come from? It comes from within.* It was a terrific race, and Eric Liddell, the "flying Scot," won the Gold Medal for the United Kingdom. And, while maintaining his faith and principles, his powerful spiritual strength clearly enhanced not only his reputation, but had a profound and positive effect on the committee, for they knew, at a much deeper level, that his position was the right one.

> *The question is not why we exist but whether we deserve to exist as supposedly rational beings ... if we act like conquerors rather than caring beings ... willing to share the planet with all those who are less powerful, and to act with restraint in respecting the needs of others and all life to come.* (Michael McCloskey)

Another terrific movie, which had a number of scenes about the power of differences, was *Dead Poets Society*, with Robin Williams, whose role was John Keating, an English teacher at a boy's boarding school. Mr. Keating asked his students to stand on his desk and *to see things differently.* At first the young men were reluctant, confused, not sure exactly what the purpose was. However, it was very clear, as they took turns looking down on the classroom, looking down on the desks, chairs, and fellow students, they were visibly moved at seeing things differently, likely for the first time; *that view was so rewarding because of its newness and its total difference from anything they had ever experienced.* They undoubtedly saw things not only with their eyes, but with their hearts, thus experiencing things differently, while gazing in its power and wonder. It was one of the defining and powerful moments of the movie.

The prominent Nobel Prize winning physicist Ilya Prigogine believed that all systems become more complex when one condition exists, namely, *excess energy to grow.* As many would have us believe, things are becoming simpler, but they are in denial. Prigogine believes we should recognize that humans are the most striking realization of the laws of nature, and we will fail if we try to make life simple. It is not. He believes the excess energy—resources, technology, competition, speed of information flow—will bring greater differences, greater diversity, and greater complexity in the world. I submit, *excess energy to grow* also includes and captures our pursuit and hunger for spiritual meaning in our lives. Differences are typically reflected in outsiders exposing us to other approaches/perspectives/ideas/options that are absolutely vital if we are to have any chance of acquiring true alignment in our lives. And outsiders can only be accessed if we embrace differences.

The diversity of mutualism, the condition where almost an infinite set of new alternatives ... new scenarios ... .new innovations ... can be generated using differences, gives us greater choices to solve the problems caused by our increasingly complex world. And, without diversity ... differences ... mutualism is impossible. (Joel Barker).

So, let's do our little quiz now. On a scale of 1-10, a score of 1 or 2 would suggest an individual who does not understand the power of *differences,* who has a deep fear, even an animosity, of people who do not look like you, do not act like you, do not think like you. In my mind, this is quite delimiting. You are never going to get close to your highest potential in life with this view. A score of 8 wold suggest you not only truly understand the power of embracing and celebrating *differences*, but your behavior reflects this view as well.

If you don't know how to behave mutalistically, if you can't collaborate with individuals and enterprises that are different from yourself, then you will never be able to reap the benefits of diversity. (Joel Barker)

Let me now invite you to explore my final *principle (#8), acquiring an appetite for personal mastery.* This *principle* brings everything together. You can aspire to greatness, if you choose. Refuse to be a *wandering generality.* Choose to be a *meaningful specific; focused, driven, passionate.* Take ownership of your life. Create your future, your destiny, your legacy.

8

ACQUIRE AN APPETITE FOR
PERSONAL MASTERY

*The thing that lights up the world and makes it bearable is
the customary feeling we have of connections with it—and
more particularly of what links us to human beings.*

— Albert Camus

So, the issue of *humanizing change* and how do we move from the "I" to
the "We"? How do we move from the "Be," the *being*, to the "Do," the
doing? Accepting change in our lives, albeit with some hesitation, is
something that most of us do fairly easily. But that's not good enough
anymore. And embracing change is likely something that we know we must
do, but have some difficulty with. That's not good enough anymore either.
Today, we must create change and then truly celebrate it. Is that easy? No,
it's difficult. But I believe it is necessary if we are to have any chance at all
to reach our highest level of potential in life.

Then, how do we take that passion—that *fire within*—to create change
and then connect to others, to the community? Thomas and Magdalen
Naylor, in their terrific book *The Search for Meaning* define community as
"a partnership of free people committed to the care and nurturing of each
other's mind, body, heart, and soul through participatory means." While I
think that about covers it all, I believe deeply that it is vital we focus, not

solely on the psychological, sociological, and financial needs we all possess, but on the spiritual as well. I think that it is the spiritual realm that we must address now, as a people, if we are to survive on this planet; or, not unlike the dinosaurs, we will become extinct, because we will have destroyed ourselves. And the first essential task is to discover what is meaningful in one's life, a team's life, or an organization's life. Thus, we need to be curious, patient, empathic listeners, keenly observant, carefully examining what we are doing while we are doing it. It cannot be done in the abstract. For it is only when we take time to discover this sense of what's worthy of our shared attention that real change occurs in our lives.

Just because an organizational leader directs or tells us that a re-design or re-structure or re-engineering is necessary, does not, in any way, compel us or inspire us to actually embrace any change. I believe this re-design and re-engineering language is a bit tired anyway. One cannot successfully take a process re-engineering, re-structuring approach to "Humanizing Change.". It doesn't work. *We really need to re-engineer how we think; and our "life becomes what our thoughts make of it."* (Marcus Aurelius). Just giving people a new, revised organizational chart, with a new set of behavioral expectations, is not going to take us to excellence. And, as far as Total Quality Management, I believe it has been an abysmal failure … because there has not been a Total Quality Culture to embrace it. *Nothing is going to change—unless and until—ideas change, and are acted upon. It's just as complicated—and just as simple—as that.*

Many, if not most of us, as I write my little book, remain in a culture that desires predictability, control, and compliance. But still no one is truly trusted, certainly not unconditionally. *It's not in the capacity of anything alive to take direction when it's trying to exercise its creativity in response to what you just asked it to do* (Margaret Wheatley). We accept it if, and only if, the experience contributes more to what we want to create, to build, and what we have defined as meaningful. And it's problematic that any culture will change internally, certainly when literally everything is happening at a faster pace than ever in our history. We are experiencing a period of desiring to be self-led, self-directed. This clearly speaks to the human need to achieve a higher level of consciousness. And, not unlike the metaphor of toothpaste coming out of the tube with the impossibility of getting it back in, once people choose to truly embrace personal empowerment that "psychological air," and feel the freedom, responsibility, and accountability that goes with it, they will absolutely reject the abusive, scorched earth, gutless, dishonest, exploitive, manipulative model of management from insecure and immature people.

An important issue regarding where we go from here is choosing to avoid one of the major exhaustion points in our lives, namely, the behavior of "just trying." Richard Flint has recently shared terrific insight into the fatigue and addiction of saying, "I'm trying" or, golly, "I tried." Trying is just not good enough because it is not doing. It's essentially a "cop out." It drains energy; it denies people their creativity. This is quite common when you are around people who do the same thing. In fact, people who consistently hide behind "I tried" look for others to reinforce and share in this type of dysfunction. Richard believes there are three reasons people buy into this behavior of "trying": one, "their life is guided by their own self-doubts"; two, "reaction has become a way of life"; they live their lives based on how they feel, on their emotions, not on principles; and thirdly, "they have years of pent-up frustrations." Do these reasons sound familiar? We have known about these ideas for many years. Why don't we choose to change? What must we do to take control of our lives; to pursue and acquire true personal mastery?

Western democracies tend to have a problem with meaning. They promise their citizens a society in which each citizen is free to create his or her own meaning—meaning which, for most of us, becomes little more than the freedom to consume at ever higher levels. (Stanley Hauerwas and William H. Willimon)

It was late summer 1973. I was a staff officer at the Defense Intelligence Agency, Arlington Hall Station, Virginia. One morning I was directed to a conference room where, along with other members of what was described as a "tiger team," we were to de-brief a number of pilots and aircrew who had been held captive in the infamous "Heartbreak Hotel," also referred to as the "Hanoi Hilton," the old French built prison in North Vietnam. Roughly 775 American Prisoners of War (POW) had been released over a period of weeks early in 1973. Many of our downed pilots and aircrew had been injured and had not been able to survive the extremely arduous trip to the Hanoi prison, from where they bailed out and were captured, with many others dying in captivity. Thus, exact numbers were not available to us.

The POW's had been released a few months prior to our de-briefings. To say I was excited is an understatement. I was truly privileged; for the next few weeks, I had the honor to meet some of the bravest, most courageous individuals one could imagine. While their spirits remained high, they had undergone horrible suffering, torture, human degradation, and deprivation. They held their heads high, proud to be in the service of their country, intensely faithful to each other, to their Commander-in-Chief, and to their country. That experience was some 29 years ago, and I will never forget it, for it left with me a deep love and appreciation for what America stands for. However, it also left me with the feeling that most of us have no idea what the potential of the human mind is. We think we know, but we do not. It is far greater than anything one could imagine. Their stories, their experiences, capture what I believe to be a "starting point" where we can begin to understand the power of discovering true *meaning in our lives, then becoming before we do.* It is "first base." And while I am choosing to leave out some of the more wretched experiences they suffered, here are a few of the remarkable stories which these true American heroes shared with my team:

- In the early years, the prisoners were severely beaten and were victims of the infamous rope torture, electric shock, brutal interrogation sessions which lasted continuously for days. They were isolated, having to survive on some 300-400 calories per day, just barely enough to sustain life. They suffered terribly from chronic diarrhea, dysentery, severe respiratory tract infections, body sores, heat rash, boils, bleeding gums. Solitary confinement, with no windows, sleeping on either boards or concrete, in six-by-six-foot cells ... were the conditions ordered for those prisoners who were the most rebellious and difficult; confinement sometimes for many months; in one instance, three and a half years. In many of their cells, the prisoners had their wrists and ankles shackled, with shackles designed for small limbs, causing extreme pain; they were also forced to live in their own body waste. And within these tight, confined enclosures, during the hot summer months in Hanoi, the temperature would reach some 120°; and in the winter, the temperature would drop down into the 20° range. Their principal weapon against this inhumanity was daily prayer and faith in their God and in their country.

- While their treatment improved in September of 1969, with the death of Ho Chi Minh, and some were able to room with other inmates, most of the physical torture ceased, but the mental torture remained and intensified. However, the North Vietnamese professional torturers were never able to destroy the POW's will to believe in their cause and their will to survive. While their physical liberty was denied them, they had the good fortune of being free; in fact, they had more freedom (of thought) than their Communist prison guards.

- During their imprisonment, they were denied any information that was favorable to America. All of the information they received from the North Vietnamese was hateful propaganda which spoke about the American military forces being destroyed on the battlefields, lies about Americans intentionally napalming innocent Vietnamese women and children, killing innocent civilians, and how much the American citizenry at home hated them and were protesting our military involvement in the war.

- The thousands of letters and care packages from loved ones during their imprisonment were rarely delivered. The prisoners were told that their nation had turned their back on them, with the North Vietnamese captors releasing information to the Red Cross that many of the POW's were actually dead, and telling some that their wives had re-married.

- Some of the most serious offenders of prison rules were literally beaten to death; many were victims of severe torture, until they became unconscious, and were then placed in appalling conditions. Solitary confinement consisted of very small rooms with no furniture, no ventilation, no lighting, for weeks at a time; POW's had to survive on meager meals of rotten meat, grass, and stale bread. Many in solitary confinement were forced to eat out of the same bowl that they used to defecate in.

- Because the need to communicate with one another was so strong, the POW's used a technique of tapping on the walls of their prison cells to talk with one another (placing the English alphabet in 25 boxes, from a to z, with c as a k, 5 letters across and 5 down). They used abbreviations, identifying the n as the word *and.* Their code, while efficient, was very time consuming, sometimes taking many hours or days just to tell of a single incident. Even though this communication was against prison rules, and the punishment was quite severe if they were caught, this important capability gave them hope, and a sense of pride and bonding with each other in their extreme suffering.

- In the evening, the Senior American Officer would initiate a tapping on the wall: the letters GBA, GOD BLESS AMERICA. Using the tapping technique, they had weekly worship service; laughed; cried; learned foreign languages; told jokes; and memorized books of the Bible, Shakespeare's Sonnets, the names of every spouse, child, pet, sibling, and parent of every inmate. Many of them designed and constructed their dream homes in their minds, and passed the designs on to their fellow prisoners. This kept their minds active and gave them a sense of hope, hope that they never lost, that they would soon be rescued. Some remain imprisoned for as long as eight years. On Sunday mornings, at roughly ten o'clock, irrespective of their faith or their religion, they would have worship services by tapping on their walls.

- They believed that human potential is unlimited; it is nothing but a state of mind. They defined it as what you believe you can do and what amount of effort you are willing to invest in order to do it. In "re-living" their lives, literally day to day, over the years they suffered in captivity, they discovered that everything that they had ever done could have been done even better.

- Although receiving minimal nutrition and despite their weakened states, they kept their bodies amazingly fit by a heavy regimen of physical exercise: jumping rope and doing pushups for hours, until they dropped from exhaustion. Until the fall of 1969, when their treatment improved, although the mental torture continued, the body weights of most of the American prisoners had dropped down to below one hundred pounds. During 1970 and 1971, while the mental torture continued, they were given more calories to consume, and many were given basic medical attention.

- The POW's told us that they went from a faith in God, to a love of God, to a knowledge of God (that *God IS*) and this knowledge gave them the strength to carry on. They had a choice of being the victim of circumstances or being empowered through them; and they chose the latter.

Their conviction was that life, even in its worst moments, had meaning; that they were free individuals who had charge over their destiny, even when the North Vietnamese guards thought they were robbing them of any shred of human hope and dignity. Their ability to find meaning in their lives, even amid terrible pain and suffering, had to be the ultimate testament to the resilience of the human spirit, a challenge to the rest of us who are not in pain or suffering at the moment. These men told me that their love and devotion to their country, America, their commitment and belief in their faith gave them the strength to carry on, to survive, when everything around them said to "give up." They drew strength from each other; they prayed for each other; they laughed, cried, felt all the human emotions together for they were never alone. *Whenever two or more are gathered in my name, I am there (Matthew 18:20).* Nothing living really lives alone. And they never stopped believing that they would eventually be released from captivity. While their liberty was denied them, they believed they had greater freedom than their captors; and this freedom was a precious blessing. These men had a vision of the future, and work left to be done, contributions still to make. They believed they served their country in very difficult circumstances, but they held their heads high.

He who loves not his country, can love nothing. (Lord George Noel Gordon Byron, 1821)

Why have I shared these terrible experiences with my readers? Life is about choices, the greatest gift that God gives us; how we choose to learn, to live, and what legacy we leave for our loved ones. Dr. Viktor Frankl provides a philosophy that is certainly relevant to life's choices: "Ultimately, man should not ask what the meaning of his life is, but rather must recognize that it is he who is asked. In a word, each man is questioned by life and he can only answer to life by answering for his own life." Thus, our behavior is a function of the choices we make, our decisions, not our conditions. The ability of these men to wrest control of their own destiny from the circumstances that surrounded them certainly showed their strength of character, their strength of duty, honor, country. But it also reflected the love they had for each other and for a mission yet to keep. They dreamed of and planned on their eventual return to America. They dreamed relentlessly, which contributed to their survival. They believed in themselves. They had a sense of belonging; for without it, there would be no soul. They held on. When everything told them to give up, they held on. They clearly had the "*fire within*."

> *Once an individual has faced the fear of looking honestly into one's own heart, he will never fear any threat that comes from outside himself again.* (*I CHING*—Chinese Book of Philosophy)

The following schema depicts various layers or stages around a core principle, *fire within*, which I believe is fundamental in understanding the possibilities and potential of acquiring true meaning and purpose in our lives. The outer circle captures the forces which touch all of us daily. The key is deciding how much *you care—about yourself, about your loved ones, about living an ethical, principle-based life, and about committing your talents and gifts to organizations that you want to serve and advance.*

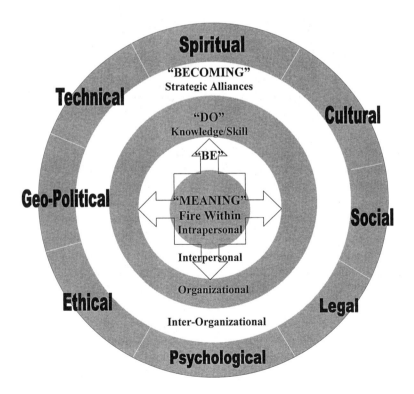

Intrapersonal

At the core; at the center of one's life is the "Fire Within," the "Passion," the foundational, fundamental "Meaning." Its most important element is the Spiritual, for we are crying out for this need to be satisfied in our lives. Choose to pursue alignment in your life; recognize its importance. "The best in art and life comes from the center ... something urgent and powerful, an idea or emotion that insists on its being. From that insistence, a shape emerges and creates its structure out of passion. If you begin with a structure, you have to make up the passion, and that's very hard to do" (Roger Rosenblatt). Internalize it; celebrate that "Fire Within." This is where it starts; and it becomes infectious, contagious. And, out of the "Fire Within", we connect with others, then discover structure. Choose to live your life based on principles of faithfulness, integrity, honor, trustworthiness, fairness, civility, and justice. Discover the one thing that breathes life into all humans—the hungry spirit, the passion. Choose not to deny, but nurture the "Fire Within." Do not censor yourself, for this violates the principle of civility and spiritual growth. For to censor yourself is cowardice, or at best, well-intentioned self-deception. Stay in alignment; stay balanced, relying on your emotional compass ... .that inner strength, that fire within. Be strong. Be courageous. A "no" uttered from the deepest conviction is better than a "yes" merely uttered to please, or what is worse, to avoid trouble (Mahandas Gandhi). Thus, choose Personal Mastery.

> *The path of Personal Mastery "is built on unrelenting practice, but it's also a place of adventure ... whether it's a sport or an art or some other work, those we call masters are shamelessly enthusiastic about their calling .... Those on the path of mastery are willing to take chances, play the fool ... . The most powerful learning is that which is more like play ... . The word generous comes from the same root as genial, generative, and genius ... . The genius has the ability to give everything, and hold nothing back. Perhaps, in fact, genius can be defined in terms of this givingness.* (George Leonard)

Interpersonal

At the next level, "Be" is the natural result of living a life based on the above cited principles. This transformational "becoming" is necessary to inspire those within your "zone of influence" to choose to transform themselves as well. This behavioral choice and commitment inspires others to self-motivate and pursue greatness in their lives, to a new state of "being." Embrace your vulnerabilities. Choose to reach out to others, engage in meaningful conversation, dialogue that breaks down barriers and removes boundaries. Choose to seek out, embrace, and celebrate differences. And "never underestimate the power of a small group of committed people to change the world. In fact, it is the only thing that ever has" (Margaret Mead). Use the true power of "choice." Rather than be limited by problems, intimidated or overwhelmed by problems and circumstances, or defeated by difficulties, make the choice to challenge, thus overcoming and conquering the issue.

Victor Parachin shared the following little story recently in his insightful research on "human potential": When an elephant is captured in Thailand, an iron band connected to a heavy chain is secured around the animal's foot. The elephant also is chained to a large tree. At first, the elephant lifts its leg and pulls, trying with all its strength to break the chain or uproot the tree, but nothing ever happens. An elephant will try this day after day, until it finally gives up. Whenever this powerful animal lifts its leg and feels just a slight tension, it drops its foot back on the ground in complete submission. Thus, after the taming period, it's quite easy to control the giant animal. The elephant then is taken out to work and is tied only to a small stake. The elephant could, with minimal effort, easily pull out the stake and run free. However, the elephant is trapped because it believes it can never break free. The creature is imprisoned simply because it perceives the situation to be impossible.

Organizational

The next level captures our power to choose to use our interpersonal skills which nurture imagination; to pursue knowledge and skills; and to be a creator; creating new paradigms and innovations. These leads to the "Doing" and "Creating" stage, which is not trying to do. It's doing and creating and meets very little resistance when one successfully achieves the "Becoming." Very few things at this stage are supported if we do not invest in creating it. This level demonstrates systems thinking, has a powerful connecting relationship to information; information actively sought and received from many sources, and the recognition of a deep connection between and among all environmental forces. It involves the issue of trust, a commitment to servant leadership, knowledge, skills, and language subtleties. Current thinking introduces the "virtual office," "virtual open organizations," virtually no hierarchy, no central offices, and an organization chart that is no longer "top down," (vertical) but a three-dimensional globe, with interconnected, internal and external profit and loss centers, to include suppliers, contractors, and sub-contractors. These collaborative networks—resilient, self-organizing systems, with a fascination for disequilibrium—will link hundreds, or even thousands, of people together in many communities, in many countries.

Rather than having dysfunctional systems, these networks are quite stable which, as described by Dr. Margaret Wheatley, "comes from a deepening center ... a deepening core ... a clarity about what it is, what it needs, what is required to survive in its environment." These networks make it possible to draw upon vital resources as needed, regardless of where they are physically and regardless of who they might be affiliated with. No constituent is ignored. Traditional offices will shrink to mere "landing sites," whose virtual stakeholders will stop in for an hour or so at a communal electric desk. Actual "face-to-face" contact will be infrequent, except for important social and fellowship purposes with colleagues. And with respect to organizational and structural intervention, "Don't ask what's wrong here ... . Ask what is possible ... and how much do you care?" (Margaret Wheatley).

Inter-Organizational

This "becoming" level captures the importance of effective strategic alliances where "win-win" value is shared. To compete in the global marketplace, "all of us are more important than any one of us." Thus, we seek meaningful relationships where the "whole is much bigger than each of the interconnected parts." As an example, the soul and spirit of a university is not found in its disparate parts and divisions. They all must be inherently inter-woven, inter-connected. Each distinct part rhythmically breathes simultaneously. And, with each heartbeat, energy flows throughout the system, like blood throughout our bodies. When one part is weak, it affects the others. Thus, the organization, the system, to reach its highest level of effectiveness, must be interdependent.

We must know that our life has value and that there is hope for our life. I have identified thirty-four areas of life's choices which I believe capture the fundamental, foundational aspects of challenging you to explore what your life is about, its meaning and purpose. I provide a "roadmap," not really to success, but to greatness. I can't promise you success, but I can promise you greatness, if you believe. It's simply entitled *CHOICES.*

1. Choose to select friends and associates who make you feel good about yourself, who lift your spirits—and avoid people who do not do this. Avoid people who literally suck the oxygen out of your lungs, denying you your creative imagination, and your sense of self-worth. Being with these people essentially reinforces and strengthens their unhappiness and misalignment. You are a VERY special and valued individual with many gifts to offer. Never forget that. "Be careful—the environment you choose will shape you; be careful—the friends you choose will result in you becoming like them" (W. Clement Stone).

2. Choose to constantly give yourself internal support and encouragement. Concentrate on positive thoughts, volunteer work, regular exercise, taking a class, listening to music or motivational disks, reading inspirational and spiritual books; anything and everything that makes you feel good about yourself. Repeat several times a day the following phrase: I am very Special and I know good things are going to happen to me today. "Our purpose, through God's Power and Love, is to support and love ourselves, support and love each other, and to shine this love outward toward the goal of bringing healing to ourselves, and to our world" (Corinne Edwards).

3. Choose to make positive, uplifting deposits in your mind, citing the many achievements and good things you have done with your life. No one has a problem-free moment in their lives, but reflect on your successes, your victories and achievements and moments of joy. Keep these memories stored for those moments when you have difficulties and challenges that are a part of the human experience. I can do all things through Christ who strengthens me (*Phillipians* 4:13).

4. Choose not to be too hard on yourself. All of us have setbacks and disappointments. This is a part of life. Remember to transform yourself; living a principle-based life is not focusing on what happens to you, but

it's how you interpret or relate to what happens to you that guides your chosen behavior. And "we do not suddenly become what we do not cooperate in becoming" (William J. Bennett).

5. Choose to grant yourself and others permission to make mistakes now and then. Making mistakes is part of life. This is what humans do, and really do quite frequently. But be mindful of the power of love and forgiveness, two fundamental principles of a self-fulfilled life. Choose never to violate those principles. To have only ourselves to love, to have no greater project in life than ourselves, is surely the very depth of meaninglessness.

6. Choose to identify your weekly priorities and keep your Life Organizer current. Include a personal journal of daily and weekly "moments of truth" which help you write your life's script … stay committed to your pursuit of greatness and your continued investment in relationships. Continually evaluate yourself realistically. "He is in possession of his life who is in possession of his story" (Carl Jung).

7. Choose to be courageous; choose never to be fearful; choose to believe that a world of love, honor, and unconditional trust truly exists. Building on Jesus' command to love thy neighbor as thyself, Eric Fromm argues that concern for the self need not necessarily be selfish. You can use all the techniques in the world, but if you don't believe in and respect yourself, truly love yourself, can you truly let go of yourself long enough to love and respect others. "Life is either a daring adventure or nothing. To keep our faces toward change and behave like free spirits in the presence of fate is strength undefeatable" (Helen Keller).

8. Choose to modify your language regarding professional and personal pursuits. Choose to avoid "tired, corrosive, immature, literally obsolete" words like … "work, job, supervisory, supervision, compliance, managers of people." Mature, cutting edge, alternative language is suggested, like "tasks, interdependence, commitments, contributions, duties, journey, service, visionary leaders, owners, creative energy, accountable stakeholders, and citizens."

9. Choose to acquire an appetite for lifelong learning. "The learned find themselves equipped to live in a world that no longer exists" (Eric Hoffer). Read outside your borders, your boundaries. Be curious about many things. Avoid people who say they are bored. These people are boring to themselves and boring to be around.

10. Choose to respect and celebrate differences; respect the uniqueness of all people. Appreciate God's gift of life. No matter how intolerable your lot, use what freedom and resources you possess to make others' lives better. "Give 24 hugs a day to those around you … just for maintenance" (Leo Buscaglia).

11. Choose to live a life of honesty and integrity, recognizing the power of preferring the uncomfortable truth over the comfortable lie; "honesty in conforming our words to reality; integrity in conforming reality to words" (Stephen Covey).

12. Choose to understand we each receive just one body. You may like it or hate it, but it will be yours for as long as you live. How you take care of it, or fail to take care of it, can make an enormous difference in the quality of your life. "Value the only companion you will have from birth to death—your self" (Eda LeShan).

13. Choose to learn lessons about life as you grow. But be mindful, lessons never end and may be different from those you think you need. "The art of being wise is the art of knowing what to overlook" (William James).

14. Choose to understand that "everything that irritates us about others can lead us to an understanding of ourselves" (Carl Jung).

15. Choose your mistakes wisely; and be mindful that one creates their patterns of behavior; their habits—then those habits create you. "It is never too late to be what you might have been" (George Eliot).

16. Choose to always remember; the secret of a life rich … and fulfilled … is love and forgiveness, which are precious gifts to ourselves. And, it's never too late to transform your life, for "you have it within your power to begin the world again" (Thomas Paine).

17. Choose to allow space for the human spirit to grow, believing that your life's purpose is something to be discovered ... and the solutions and answers to all of life's problems lie within your grasp. "Man is the only animal who has to be encouraged to live" (Friedrich Nietzsche).

18. Choose not to be casual about life; for if you do, you will surely become a casualty! Stay focused. Become relentless as you pursue your dreams. "Showing up is 95% of life," (Andy Warhol) and the other 5% is persistence. "Great works are performed, not by strength, but by perseverance" (Samuel Johnson). "Our plans miscarry because they have no aim. When a man does not know what harbor he is making for, no wind is the right wind" (Marcus Annaeus Seneca).

19. Choose to define courage not as the absence of fear, but as the presence of faith. "The only failure a man ought to fear is failure in cleaving to the purpose he sees to be best" (George Eliot).

20. Choose to respect and recognize the beauty and wonder of our creation and the majesty and beauty of our land, which we inherit from our parents and leave to our children.

21. Choose to believe in the power and gift of human imagination, creativity and fully appreciate the expansive capacity of all humans. Internalize the possibility of possibilities. To resist change is an act against life; and all of life resists control. "The highest reward for a person's toil is not what they get for it, but what they become by it" (John Ruskin).

22. Choose to respect and recognize the fragility of life, our mortality, our race against death, but a race worthy of the best in all of us. Every moment of one's existence one is growing into more or retreating into less. One is always living a little more ... or dying a little bit" (Norman Mailer).

23. Choose to believe in the power of humility, always questioning your motives, and believe "the strongest principle of growth lies in human choice" (George Eliot).

24. Choose, in all relationships, to have faith and exercise unconditional trust ... knowing and accepting the fact that, as humans, we quite often deceive ourselves and others. My friends, this is tough, but, potentially, life changing.

25. Choose to be a "top performer"; otherwise, find something else to do! Rather than being designed by your experience, be your own designer. "You become cause AND effect rather than mere effect. Self-aware-ness = Self-knowledge = Self-possession = Self-control = Self expression. You make your life your own by understanding it" (Warren Bennis).

26. Choose to truly appreciate and respect language, commiting oneself to empathic listening. "While the right to talk is the beginning of freedom, the necessity of listening is what makes that right important" (Walter Lippman).

27. Choose to accept the fact that everything you have ever done in your life, you know you could have done a little bit better; and your potential for growth relies solely on what you think you can do, and the amount of investment/effort you are willing to put into that process.

28. Choose to respect and appreciate the gift of life. Invest in and take care of yourself. "The body is a sacred garment. It's your first and last garment; it is what you enter life in and what you depart life with, and it should be treated with honor" (Martha Graham).

29. Choose to believe that extraordinary achievements can be attained by ordinary people.

30. Choose to be a person of faith, expressing and reflecting devotion to one's deity. "And he will raise you up on Eagle's wings, bear you on the breath of dawn, make you shine like the sun, and hold you in the palm of his hand" (*Isaiah* 40:31).

31. Choose never to have another bad day in your life. (However accept the fact that some days are a little bit better than others.)

32. Choose to reflect deeply on the wisdom of learning, unlearning, and relearning. (Alvin Toffler)

33. Choose to wonder how you ever got this far in life without considering these choices.

34. Choose not to forget this list of "choices," for, if you do, everything you have just read won't mean a thing.

It is strongly suggested that you have big dreams. *Dr Martin Luther King, Jr., didn't say "I have an idea". He said, "I have a Dream."* How many people actually write down their dreams; apparently, according to researchers who worry about these things, only about three percent of us. And, although we might think about "dreams," we don't write them down. So that leaves some ninety-seven percent of Americans just wandering through life, bumping into things, responding and reacting to other people's expectations and assumptions about their roles and goals in life. How sad, how discouraging. Choose to write down your dreams. They can become a contract. Anais Nin describes dreams that "pass into the reality of action; and from the action, stems the dream again—and this interdependence produces the highest form of living." Another unknown author wrote:

Dream Big

If there were ever a time to date, to make a difference, to embark on something worth doing, it is now. Not for any grand cause, necessarily, but for something that tugs at your heart, something that's your aspiration, something that's your dream.

You owe it to yourself to make your days here count. Have fun. Dig deep. Stretch. Dream big.

Know, though, that things worth doing seldom come easy. There will be good days. And there will be bad days. There will be times when you want to turn around, pack it up, and call it quits. Those times will tell you that you are pushing yourself, that you are not afraid to learn by trying. Persist.

Because with an idea, determination, and the right tools, you can do great things. Let your instincts, your intellect, your heart guide you. Trust.

Believe in the incredible power of the human mind. Of doing something that makes a difference. Of working hard. Of laughing and hoping. Of lazy afternoons. Of lasting friends. Of all the things that will cross your path this year.

The start of something new brings the hope of something great. Anything is possible. There is only one you. And you will pass this way only once. Do it right.

We pass this way only once. And today you've got one big shot. For tomorrow, today is in the dust pan of history, gone forever. *Drop the question what tomorrow may bring, and count as profit every day that fate allows you (Horace).* Life is about choices. That's all, just choices: a choice to be good, or be bad; a choice to do the right thing, or the wrong thing; a choice to care, not care, trust, or not trust. Somehow in this new millennium, we have created lives that are exceedingly busy, leaving little time for the great questions of *belonging.* These questions, spoken or not spoken, lie at the center of what gives a human being a sense of meaning and purpose.

I suggest we first must discover, or recover, what is already there, not create, but discover our life's *meaning,* the *doing,* then the *be* as we approach and enter the *becoming* stage of enlightenment. Afterwards, we acknowledge and celebrate the *do* stage of action and behavior and the cycle starts over with the *becoming.* Even in death, the cycle continues with our love ones, our neighbors, our co-workers, our students, whom we may have influenced. Dr. Magdalena Taylor has stated that *the whole purpose of psychotherapy is to teach the patient how to be."* Thus, it is only through *discovering "meaning" in our lives, then advancing through the "be" and "becoming" stages that we define who we are.* Ultimately, it's the human spirit and our hunger for meaning in our lives, our search for and need to connect with others, as we commit ourselves to a life of service. Processes don't think; technologies don't act. And the organizational world is more like a complex living ecosystem. Only humans can think deeply, dream, innovate, imagine, and pursue greatness. But for this to happen, we must have freedom to grow, and we must have an economic system that lubricates the process.

According to Professor Thomas Donaldson at the University of Virginia, we must remember that the economic system that continues to serve us so well is relatively new. It is only about two centuries old, and like any social system it does not remain static but undergoes constant evolutionary transformation. He believes there have been two stages to the ensuing revolution. *The first stage involved the law,* and it is one which is largely complete. The *second* one, in which we are directly involved is a more *difficult transformation that involves a belief that all of us, by our choices, can truly create our legacies, our destinies, our futures.* And this stage has really just begun. But, I hasten to add, we are truly blessed to have a form of social-political organization, a representative democratic form of government, that has demonstrated extreme resilience under conditions of constant change and turbulence.

> *Both the economic system and the political system in America will only be maintained over time to the degree that there is individual goodwill, virtuous living and cooperation. Otherwise, both systems will be destroyed; the political and the economic.* (Adam Smith)

I believe this turbulent, even strange, changing world requires dealing with a great deal of confusion and uncertainty; and to survive, one has to acquire an appetite for creative imagination, curiosity, courage, and commitment. I don't believe a person can be truly creative if they refuse to be confused on occasion. Transition, which is psychological, precedes change. And change itself always begins with some degree of being confused, disoriented, uncertain. But you must work this stage. Don't fear it. Look deep within yourself for meaning in your life. Stay focused, balanced, believe, learn, live, love, and serve.

> *Speaking of the tension between freedom, power and perfection on the one hand and imperfection, impotence, and imprisonment on the other .... isn't this what life is all about? It seems to me the human condition is most basically that we are willful creatures living in a world that, much of the time, doesn't behave the way we want it to. We live in the tension between our will and reality. Sometimes with great effort and expertise, we can change reality or bend it to our will. At other times—also with great effort and*

expertise—it is we who must change by coming to accept the limitations of the world and of ourselves. (M. Scott Peck)

But be not afraid. Be brave. *For God has not given us a spirit of fear, but of power and of love (Timothy* 1:7).

Whoever loves money never has money enough; whoever loves wealth is never satisfied with [one's] income. This, too ... is meaningless. As goods increase, so do those who consume them. And what benefit are they to the owner except to feast [one's] eyes on them? (Ecclesiastes 5:10-11)

So, how would you score on a scale of 1-10, one being an individual who truly is out of alignment, not anchored, not centered. A score above 8 would suggest you are on your way to greatness. Enjoy. Let me share my final piece to the puzzle, my *epilogue.* I invite you to explore the highest level you can attain, one of pure joy and fulfillment. (Note the following wisdom from *1 Corinthians,* 13)

If I speak in the tongues of men and of angels, but have not love, I am a noisy gong or a clanging cymbal. And if I have prophetic powers, and understand all mysteries and all knowledge, and if I have all faith, so as to remove mountains, but have not love, I am nothing. If I give away all I have, and if I deliver my body to be burned, but have not love, I gain nothing.

Love is patient and kind; love is not jealous or boastful; it is not arrogant or rude. Love does not insist on its own way; it is not irritable or resentful; it does not rejoice at wrong, but rejoices in the right. Love bears all things, believes all things, hopes all things, endures all things.

Love never ends; as for prophecies, they will pass away; as for tongues, they will cease; as for knowledge, it will pass away. For our knowledge is imperfect and our prophecy is imperfect; but when the perfect comes, the imperfect will pass away. When I was a child, I spoke like a child. I thought like a child, I reasoned like a child; when I became a man, I gave up childish ways. For now we see in a mirror dimly, but then face to face. Now I know in part;

then I shall understand fully, even as I have been fully understood. So faith, hope, love abide, these three; but the greatest of these is love.

Let me now invite you to read my Epilogue, which brings to closure this journey of exploration and discovery. I trust that you will reflect upon and process the words, reading not only with your eyes, but with your heart. It has been a journey of risk, but worth taking; a journey of examining what the miracle of life is about, what potential rests within all of us. Choose to be great today.

EPILOGUE

It remains my strong conviction that by the end of this decade, the paradigmatic changes that will occur ... and affect virtually all institutions, will be seen as more radical than any human can now possibly propose or anticipate.

— Travis L. Sample

As we entered the 21st century, optimism was seen everywhere. We had overcome and lived through the turbulent, but "go-go 90's," a decade that gave us an emotional roller coaster. We experienced the breakup of the Soviet Union, the destruction of the Berlin Wall, and the peaking and implosion of the "dot-com" phenomena. And, because of an increasing acceptance and celebration of the powerful freedom of choices in our lives, the rules were forced to change in the workplace. Uncertainty, not initially accepted as the creative tool it is meant to be, was introduced universally to our DNA. Instability, insecurity, uncertainty became a part of our daily lives. I suggest that what used to scare and threaten us, we now accept as vital to our shared humanity and not only for increased prosperity, but literally for our survival. We had forgotten that we are all interrelated, sharing the same value, and that we are on this earth for each other.

But, as I write this Epilogue, the world seems spinning out of control. The horrific events of September 11, 2001 have truly changed the world. America is in the midst of a World War, a different kind of war, a war we did not seek, or plan for. But our great country will successfully end this conflict on a date and on terms that we will choose. The Middle East is in crisis, and the future is quite troublesome. We are left with the aching, sickening feeling in the pit of our stomachs as to whether the human race on this earth will survive this century, or this decade. Only time will tell.

With a half-billion people on the globe using the Internet daily, and projections that the number of users will triple by the end of this decade, with many of us already suffering from information "overload," how can we possibly relate to the paradigmatic changes that will be occurring, challenging all of us to stay in alignment, to stay centered, balanced? Tom Peters, always ready for a quick dose of wisdom, shared the following, cogent analysis. *"GOK": God only knows.* But, I suggest we stay focused and not be spectators. Life is too short.

With respect to what worries most organizations today, Tom Peters says, "*There is both good and bad news. The good news is that they do not see survival as automatic. The bad news is that they are uniformly unwilling to embark on a journey of total transformation.*" I believe this will not occur, unless and until each of us commits ourself to *self-transformation.* It's just that simple or just that complicated.

> *For every one that asketh, receiveth; and he that seeketh, findeth; and to him that knocketh it shall be opened.* (*Matthew* 7:7-8)

Humanizing Change relies on personal courage, embracing that *fire within* and choosing to transform your life. For to operationalize and act upon my *eight principles* will be a significant challenge for you. You might likely first find those close associates/friends around you or those in your organization *resisting* behavior that you have chosen to adopt, reluctant to be more creative, imaginative, and passionate in their personal as well as professional lives. For those individuals, the *fire within* has not been lit. After this *resistance* stage, you will observe and experience individuals who might *ridicule* you, singling you out as a "show boat," or "show off." Be courageous. Be fearless. It's not what people do to you that hurts you. It's *how you relate to* and *interpret* what people do to you that eventually and potentially can hurt you. *Do the thing you fear and the death of fear is certain (Ralph Waldo Emerson).*

Choose not to empower others' dysfunction, insecurity, and immaturity. Then, after the *ridiculing*, you may sense *anger* in those around you who do not choose to embrace and celebrate change in their lives, and in the organization they are affiliated with. This *anger* might even be personally directed at you, or used by immature and insecure people, in an attempt to hurt you by manipulating others around you. Following *anger*, you might observe *oppression*, a concerted effort to suppress the changes, hoping things will return to normalcy. And, finally, following the oppression stage, you will be rewarded, recognized, then given *respect*. And, as this stage continues and increases in power, others will be influenced greatly by your courage and choose to transform themselves. Thus, be a model; be an example. *The best way to predict your future is to create it (Erich Fromm).*

It had been less than a year since man first walked on the moon, but as far as the American public was concerned, *Apollo 13,* launched in 1973, was just another routine space flight, but, as we recall, it was surely not routine. It also became, in 1995, a fabulous movie, based on the true depiction of a crippled spacecraft. The astronauts were Jim Lovell, portrayed by Tom Hanks; Fred Haise, portrayed by Bill Paxton; and Jack Swigert, portrayed by Kevin Bacon. While the story was one of courage, faith, and ingenuity, what really struck me, as an analog, was what happened during the first 12 minutes 34 seconds of the flight. Virtually 99% of all the energy required for the four-day mission was expended in the first 12 minutes, 34 seconds. At that moment, they broke totally free of earth's gravity. All resistance was behind them. To me, this powerfully communicates that, as you internalize and actualize my *eight principles*, you are going to predictably experience some turbulence, uncertainty, confusion, and self-doubt. Expect it. Don't avoid it. However, when you break free of that toxic, corrosive feeling, freeing yourself from being held back, not reaching your highest level of potential, then it becomes a different life, one far more fulfilling and glorious.

For surely, I know the plans I have for you, says the Lord, plans for your welfare and not for harm, to give you a future with hope. (Jeremiah 29:11)

Choose today to discover and recover that *fire within*, the true meaning in your life. Choose to grasp onto and release the un-tapped potential that you have within you. Believe in yourself. Look for those relationships/opportunities that will excite you, inspiring you to be the very best you can be, in all of life's roles. *"Four things come now back; the spoken word, the sped arrow, the past, and the neglected opportunity" (Omar Idn Al-Halif).* Choose to take this opportunity and transform your life. Live a life based on that *fire within*; live a life based on pursuing your dreams in life, a life committed to investing heavily in relationships and serving the larger community, the larger good. And be mindful, that no relationship can survive and mature unless you are prepared to trust, to trust unconditionally and to continue to trust when that trust is violated. Is this tough or easy? It is brutually difficult, but so rewarding. If you choose never to forgive, it is problematic that you can ever achieve positive, fulfilling, valued relationships.

The wisdom and insight of Thomas Carlyle is so true today; *The ideal is in thyself, the impediment, too, is in thyself.* Choose not to be reticent, timid. A new world is beckoning. Choose to change your paradigm, reflecting upon, internalizing and actualizing my *eight principles*, and you will have changed your life.

I suspect that very little of what I have shared with you in my little book was new to you. For I have just reminded you of things you already know. The important issue, though, is to choose to live a life which adheres to and embraces my principles, rather than just being familiar with them. If you choose to believe in *and act upon* my *eight principles for acquiring true personal and professional excellence,* and this is not hyperbole, it is *potentially life-changing.* Your paradigm, your mental map, will change. You will see and experience a different world. Your relationships will be more complete, more fulfilled, more spiritually alive. People in your *zone of peace—that space which surrounds you, that energy which draws people to you, not unlike a magnet—will start treating you differently.* They will watch you when you do not know they are observing you. They will listen to you when you are not aware they are listening to you. There really are no secrets to personal transformation. It fundamentally rests with satisfying basic spiritual needs.

> *The four basic spiritual needs felt by human beings are deep needs to have a sense of: uniqueness as an individual; union with something greater than the self; usefulness to others; and understanding about our lives and work.* (Tom Morris)

Choose no longer to be a victim; choose not to sit back and react to other people's expectations and assumptions about your roles and goals in life. Choose to be courageous, no longer betraying yourself and the value you place upon yourself as a truly unique human being. Life is precious. Choose to pursue your dreams, to rely on those skills, competencies, and tools which challenge you daily to be your very best. Choose not to rely solely on those achievements that you have already mastered. Growth is a personal choice and is a journey, not a destination. Love that truly amazing and glorious aspect of the human experience, the marvelous opportunity to search for, discover, and connect with your inner soul; then create your personal transformation.

Find a quiet, private place to look deep within your inner soul. Relax and compose yourself. Close your eyes. Embrace your emotions, one of God's gifts to man. When asked by Barbara Walters, why he was so open and free with his emotions, Norman Schwarzkopf, one of our nation's great military leaders, said *he doesn't trust a man who can't cry.* You must connect your private life with your deep inner life, for that is where the most significant decisions of your life will be made. It's your choice. Rely upon and believe in that *fire within.* Embrace the view that one is both responsible and accountable for their growth, their life, and ultimate destiny. What legacy will you live? Choose to pursue greatness today. Mean it. Do it. Become; then become reborn again. Live life to its fullest. Carpe Diem!

An Irish Blessing

May the road rise up to meet you.
May the wind always be at your back.
May the sun shine warm upon your face.
The rain fall soft upon your fields.
And, until we meet again,
May God hold you in the hollow of his hand.

RECOMMENDED READING

Aubrey, Robert and Paul M. Cohen; *Working Wisdom*

Autry, James; *Love and Profit, and Life and Work*

Bennett, William J.; *The Moral Compass and the Book of Virtues*

Bennis, Warren; *On Becoming A Leader*

Buscaglia, Leo; *Born for Love and Love*

Cooper, Robert; *Executive EQ, and The Other 90%: How To Unlock Your Vast Hidden Potential For Leadership and Life*

Covey, Stephen R.; *The Seven Habits of Highly Effective People, First Things First and Principle Centered Leadership*

Etzioni, Amitai; *The Spirit of Community*

Fairholm, Gilbert W.; *Leadership and The Culture of Trust*

Frankl, Viktor; *Man's Search for Meaning*

Fukuyama, Francis; *Trust*

Handy, Charles; *The Hungry Spirit*

Hillman, James; *The Soul's Code: In Search of Character and Calling*

Katzenbach, Jon R.; *Real Change Leaders*

Kidder, Rushworth M. ed.; *Shared Values for a Troubled World*

Kouzes, James M. and Barry Z. Posner; *Encouraging the Heart*

Lee, Blaine; *The Power Principle*

Lipman-Blumen, Jean and Harold J. Leavitt; *Hot Groups and Connective Leadership*

Lundin, Stephen C. and Marshall Goldsmith; *Feedback is A Gift*

Marshall, Edward; *Building Trust at the Speed of Change*

Nanus, Burt; *The Leader's Edge*

Manz, Charles C. and Christopher P. Neck; *Mastering Self-Leadership: Empowering Yourself For Personal Excellence*

Peck, M. Scott; *The Road Less Traveled, A World Waiting To Be Born, Further Along The Road Less Traveled, and Golf and the Spirit*

Peters, Tom; *The Circle of Innovation and We Are In A Brawl With No Rules*

Rifkin, Jeremy; *The End of Work*

Scherer, John; *Work and the Human Spirit*

Senge, Peter; *The Fifth Discipline Fieldbook, and the Dance of Change*

Smith, Hyrum W.; *What Matters Most: The Power of Living Your Values*

Welch, Jack; *Jack Welch and the GE Way and Jack—Straight from the Gut*

Wheatley, Margaret J., *Leadership and the New Science*

Wheatley, Margaret J. and Myron Kellner-Rogers; *a simpler way*

Whyte, David; *The Heart Aroused*

INDEX

ABOUT THE AUTHOR

Dr. Travis L. Sample, an acclaimed inspirational speaker, is Founder and President of *Travis Sample Seminars*, and a Professor of Business Administration at Shenandoah University. He has a B.S. in Psychology and Sociology from the University of Houston; an M.S. in Government from Southern Illinois University; an M.P.A. from the University of Southern California (USC), and a Doctorate in Public Administration from USC, with concentrations in Organizational Theory and Behavior. A retired Air Force Colonel, Travis lives in Leesburg, Virginia with his wife, Barbara, and can be reached at http://www.humanizingchange.com